The Ultimate Cuisinart Air Fryer Oven Cookbook

350 Easy & Delicious Recipes to Air fry, Bake, Broil and Toast

(for Beginners and Advanced Users)

Grace Lecompte

Table of Contents

Introduction 7

    Why this cookbook? 7

    Functions and Benefits 7

Breakfast Recipes 8

    Banana & Peanut Butter Cake 8

    Apricot Scones with Almonds 8

    Vanilla Brownies with White Chocolate & Walnuts 9

    Savory Cheddar & Cauliflower Tater Tots 9

    Raspberries Maple Pancakes 10

    Nutmeg Potato Gratin 10

    Cheesy Eggs with Fried Potatoes 10

    Crunchy Asparagus with Cheese 11

    Breaded Cauliflowers in Alfredo Sauce 11

    Lemon Vanilla Cupcakes with Yogurt Frost 11

    Creamy Vanilla Berry Mini Pies 12

    Olive & Tomato Tart with Feta Cheese 12

    Buttery Cheese Sandwich 13

    Creamy Bacon & Egg Wraps with Spicy Salsa 13

    Corn & Chorizo Frittata 13

    Yogurt & Cream Cheese Zucchini Cakes 14

    Prosciutto & Salami Egg Bake 14

    Almond & Cinnamon Berry Oat Bars 15

    Cinnamon Mango Bread 15

    Cheesy Potato & Spinach Frittata 15

    Caprese Sandwich with Sourdough Bread 16

    Cheddar Cheese Hash Browns 16

    Creamy Parmesan & Ham Shirred Eggs 17

    Creamy Mushroom and Spinach Omelet 17

    Spinach & Kale Balsamic Chicken 17

    Tasty Cheddar Omelet 18

    Classic Bacon & Egg English Muffin 18

    Salty Parsnip Patties 18

    Giant Strawberry Pancake 19

Quick Paprika Eggs 19

Parsley Onion & Feta Tart 19

Classic Cheddar Cheese Omelet 20

Tomato, Basil & Mozzarella Breakfast 20

Fresh Kale & Cottage Omelet 20

Buttered Apple & Brie Cheese Sandwich 21

Herby Parmesan Bagel 21

Vanilla & Cinnamon Toast Toppet 21

Cinnamon-Orange Toast 22

Prosciutto & Mozzarella Crostini 22

Porridge with Honey & Peanut Butter 22

Peppery Sausage & Parsley Patties 23

Honey Banana Pastry with Berries 23

Appetizers & Side Dishes 24

    Homemade Tortilla Chips 24

    Sweet Pickle Chips with Buttermilk 24

    Grandma's Apple Cinnamon Chips 24

    Crunchy Cheese Twists 25

    Mixed Nuts with Cinnamon 25

    Garlicky Mushroom Spaghetti 25

    Cheese Eggplant Boats with Ham & Parsley 26

    Goat Cheese & Pancetta Bombs 26

    Delicious Chicken Wings with Alfredo Sauce 26

    Mini Salmon Quiches 27

    Perfect Crispy Potatoes 27

    Egg Roll Wrapped with Cabbage & Prawns 27

    Cheesy Sticks with Thai Sauce 28

    Jalapeno Popper Chicken with Bacon 28

    Maple Shrimp with Coconut 29

    Sesame Garlic Chicken Wings 29

    Whole Chicken with BBQ Sauce 30

    Cheesy Crisps 30

    Allspice Chicken Wings 30

Pineapple Pork Ribs...31

Parsley Mushroom Pilaf..31

Savory Chicken Nuggets with Parmesan Cheese..........31

Dill Pickles with Parmesan 32

Grandma's Chicken Thighs.....................................32

Homemade Cod Fingers...32

Stuffed Mushrooms with Rice & Cheese.....................33

Party Chicken Wings 33

Creamy Eggplant Cakes...34

Thyme & Carrot Cookies 34

Garlic Lemon Roasted Chicken 34

Chickpeas with Rosemary & Sage 35

Crispy Onion Rings with Buttermilk 35

Easy Crunchy Garlic Croutons.................................35

Traditional French Fries 36

Gourmet Beef Sticks 36

Simple Chicken Breasts 36

Cabbage Wedges with Parmesan.............................37

Crispy Calamari Rings 37

Homemade Cheesy Sticks......................................37

Party Macaroni Quiche with Greek Yogurt..................37

Feta Lime Corn 38

Bacon & Potato Salad with Mayonnaise 38

Garlic Potato Chips 38

Spicy Pumpkin-Ham Fritters 39

Holiday Pumpkin Wedges 39

Savory Parsley Crab Cakes 40

Ham Rolls with Vegetables & Walnuts 40

Potato Chips with Lemony Dip..................................40

Bok Choy Crisps 41

Amul Cheesy Cabbage Canapes...............................41

Feta Butterbeans with Crispy Bacon 41

French Beans with Toasted Almonds 42

Shrimp with Spices..42

Bacon Wrapped Asparagus 42

Brussels Sprouts with Garlic....................................43

Yogurt Masala Cashew...43

Simple Parmesan Sandwich.....................................43

Savory Curly Potatoes 44

Tasty Carrot Chips 44

French-Style Fries 44

Cheese & Chive Scones 44

Pineapple & Mozzarella Tortillas 45

Marinara Chicken Breasts 45

Easy Parsnip Fries 45

Air Fried Mac & Cheese 46

Homemade Cheddar Biscuits 46

Molasses Cashew Delight 46

Ham and Cheese Grilled Sandwich............................47

Crispy Eggplant Fries 47

Homemade Prosciutto Wrapped Cheese Sticks............47

Mom's Tarragon Chicken Breast Packets.....................47

Poultry Recipes 49

Marinara Sauce Cheese Chicken...............................49

Honey & Garlic Chicken Thighs.................................49

Parmesan Chicken Fingers with Plum Sauce 49

Herby Chicken with Lime...50

Spicy Chicken Strips with Aioli Sauce 50

Fried Chicken Tenderloins 51

Ham & Cheese Stuffed Chicken Breasts 51

Chicken Wrapped in Bacon 51

Thyme Turkey Nuggets...52

Cayenne Chicken Drumsticks...................................52

Fruity Chicken Breasts with BBQ Sauce 52

Herby Stuffed Turkey Breast 53

Mango Marinated Chicken Breasts.............................53

Sticky Chinese-Style Chicken...................................54

Worcestershire Chicken Breasts................................54

Korean-Style Chicken Wings 55

Savory Honey & Garlic Chicken 55

Shrimp Paste Chicken..55

Sherry Grilled Chicken 56

Hot Chicken Wings 56

Pineapple & Ginger Chicken Kabobs 56

Mustardy Chicken 57

Sweet Chicken Drumsticks 57

Chicken with Peppercorns & Lemon 58

Cheesy Chicken Escallops 58

Savory Buffalo Chicken 58

Garlic-Buttery Chicken Wings 59

Rosemary Chicken Breasts 59

Enchilada Cheese Chicken 59

Basil Mozzarella Chicken 60

Lime-Chili Chicken Wings 60

Chicken with Avocado & Radish Bowl 60

Delicious Coconut Chicken Casserole 61

Savory Chicken with Onion 61

Basil Cheese Chicken 61

Cayenne Chicken with Coconut Flakes 62

Honey Chicken Wings 62

Ginger Chicken Wings 62

Parmesan Chicken Cutlets 63

Buttered Crispy Turkey 63

Meat Recipes 64

Homemade Pork Ratatouille 64

Sweet Marinaded Pork Chops 64

Beef Rolls with Pesto & Spinach 64

Savory Pulled Pork with Cheddar & Bacon 65

Italian-Style Pork Chops 65

Tamarind Pork Chops with Green Beans 66

Almond & Apple Pork Balls 66

Teriyaki Pork Ribs with Tomato Sauce 66

Corned Beef with Carrots 67

Chili Pork Chops with Tomatoes & Rice 67

Cocktail Franks in Blanket 68

Smoked Ham with Pears 68

Morning Ham & Cheese Sandwich 68

Sage Sausage Balls 69

Cheese Breaded Pork 69

Pork Belly with Honey 69

Grandma's Ground Beef Balls 70

Swiss Cheese Ham Muffins 70

Amazing Bacon & Potato Platter 70

Party Stuffed Pork Chops 71

Cheddar Pork Meatballs 71

Fish & Seafood Recipes 72

Cheesy Tilapia Fillets 72

Simple Lemon Salmon 72

Chili-Rubbed Jumbo Shrimp 72

Rosemary Buttered Prawns 73

Parmesan Fish with Pine Nuts 73

Delightful Catfish Fillets 73

Shrimp with Smoked Paprika & Cayenne Pepper 74

Speedy Fried Scallops 74

Fried Cod Nuggets 74

Savory Cod Fish in Soy Sauce 75

Crispy Crab Legs 75

Quick Shrimp Bowl 75

Garlic-Butter Catfish 76

Delicious Fried Seafood 76

Easy Salmon Cakes 76

Old Bay Tilapia Fillets 77

Sweet Cajun Salmon 77

Lemon-Garlic Butter Lobster 77

Meatless Recipes 78

Sandwiches with Tomato, Nuts & Cheese 78

Vegetable Fried Mix Chips 78

Cayenne Spicy Green Beans 79

Cheesy Cabbage Wedges 79

Traditional Jacket Potatoes 79

Roasted Carrots 80

Garlicky Veggie Bake..80

Sweet Baby Carrots...80

Colorful Vegetarian Delight 81

Awesome Sweet Potato Fries............................81

Rosemary Butternut Squash Roast...................81

Herby Tofu...82

Cheesy Frittata with Vegetables......................82

Cauliflower Rice with Tofu & Peas...................83

Chickpea & Carrot Balls 83

Yummy Chili Bean Burritos................................84

Tasty Polenta Crisps 84

Garlicky Fennel Cabbage Steaks 84

Simple Ricotta & Spinach Balls 85

Baby Spinach & Pumpkin with Nuts & Cheese.............85

Mom's Blooming Buttery Onion 85

Mozzarella Eggplant Patties 86

Parsley Feta Triangles 86

Broccoli & Cheese Egg Ramekins 86

Zucchini Parmesan Crisps.................................87

Cheese with Spinach Enchiladas 87

Vegetable Au Gratin 88

Russian-Style Eggplant Caviar 88

Vegetable Spring Rolls......................................88

Speedy Vegetable Pizza....................................89

Cumin and Cayenne Spicy Sweet Potatoes...................89

Jalapeño & Tomato Gratin 90

Chili Veggie Skewers 90

Classic Ratatouille 91

Cheddar & Tempeh Stuffed Mushrooms 91

Korean Tempeh Steak with Broccoli.................91

Parsley Hearty Carrots 92

Homemade Cheese Ravioli.................................92

Beetroot Chips 93

Coconut Vegan Fries..93

Garlicky Vermouth Mushrooms 93

Desserts Recipes **94**

Summer Citrus Sponge Cake 94

Vanilla Brownie Squares 94

Effortless Apple Pie...95

Dark Chocolate Lava Cakes 95

Perfect Chocolate Soufflé 95

Glazed Lemon Cupcakes 96

Homemade Doughnuts 96

Sesame Banana Dessert....................................97

Triple Berry Lemon Crumble 97

Honey Hazelnut Apples 97

French Apple Cake 98

Classic Pecan Pie 98

Authentic Raisin Apple Treat.............................99

Crumble with Blackberries & Apricots........................99

Quick Coffee Cake 99

Gluten-Free Fried Bananas..............................100

Vanilla Almond Cookies....................................100

Introduction

If you want to whip up delicious, nutritious, tasty meals with a single touch of a button, you need an oven that can toast and air fry. The Cuisinart Air Fryer Toaster Oven does just that - it serves not only as an air frier but also as a fast and efficient electric oven and a toaster. Spend less time in your kitchen and enjoy your loved ones while the marvelous Cuisinart cooks some crispy chicken with french fries. It can also broil, bake, or warm, and all this in a single kitchen appliance. A little too much information for you? Don't worry, as this cookbook will guide you through the process of taking advantage of your cooking appliance.

Cuisinart Air Fryer Toaster Oven is a unique kitchen machine, and a full-size toasting oven with an air fryer built-in. So, it not only broils, bakes and toasts, but it will also let you air fry right inside the oven. With the air frying function, you can cook delicious fried meals, such as wings, fritters, fries, or shrimp, more healthily, thanks to its powerful hot-air technology. Say bye to messy cleanups and say hi to crunchy and crispy experiences without the extra calories, with the new Cuisinart Air Fryer Toaster Oven.

Why this cookbook?

This cookbook encompasses a wide variety of recipes that are easy to follow and, most importantly, very easy to cook inside your Air Fryer oven. This book is meant to be a guide to you as you explore the novelty of the Cuisinart Air Fryer Oven. My goal is that you will be able to make some sumptuous meals without the pain of spending many hours in the kitchen. You will find that the ingredients used here are easy to find, and the cooking process is straightforward. Most of the recipes cook in less than one hour, which is the main reason this kitchen appliance was invented - to cook faster than a traditional oven.

Functions and Benefits

Power on Light - This Indicator lights up when in use

ON/Oven Timer Dial - Use to set desired time for all functions except Toast function. Setting the oven timer powers the unit on and begins the cooking cycle. When the timer runs out, the unit will power off.

Oven Temperature Dial - set the temperature desired

Function Dial - select the cooking settings – Warm, Bake, Broil, Air Fry, etc.

ON/Toast Timer Dial - choose desired toasting shade from lighter to darker.

Pull Out Crumb Tray - it comes positioned inside the oven. It comes out from the bottom front of the oven for convenient cleaning.

Air Fryer Basket - use the basket on Air Fry setting for optimal cooking outcome. Always use nested in the baking pan.

Oven Rack - use in two positions: bottom or top.

Drip Tray/Baking Bpan - this equipment is included in the package. Use it when or roasting or baking, and with the frying basket when Air Frying.

Breakfast Recipes

Banana & Peanut Butter Cake

Prep + Cook Time: 30 minutes | Serves: 4

1 cup flour

¼ tsp baking soda

1 tsp baking powder

⅓ cup sugar

2 mashed bananas

¼ cup vegetable oil

1 egg, beaten

1 tsp vanilla extract

¾ cup chopped walnuts

¼ tsp salt

2 tbsp peanut butter

2 tbsp sour cream

Directions

Preheat Cuisinart on Bake function to 350 F. Spray a 9-inch baking pan with cooking spray or grease with butter. Combine the flour, salt, baking powder, and baking soda in a bowl.

In another bowl, combine bananas, oil, egg, peanut butter, vanilla, sugar, and sour cream. Combine both mixtures gently. Stir in the chopped walnuts. Pour the batter into the pan. Cook for 20 minutes. Let cool completely and serve sliced.

Apricot Scones with Almonds

Prep + Cook Time: 30 minutes | Serves: 4

Ingredients

2 cups flour

⅓ cup sugar

2 tsp baking powder

½ cup sliced almonds

¾ cup chopped dried apricots

¼ cup cold butter, cut into cubes

½ cup milk

1 egg

1 tsp vanilla extract

Directions

Line a large baking sheet with parchment paper. Mix together flour, sugar, baking powder, almonds, and apricots. Rub the butter into the dry ingredients with hands to form a sandy, crumbly texture. Whisk together egg, milk, and vanilla extract.

Pour into the dry ingredients and stir to combine. Sprinkle a working board with flour, lay the dough onto the board and give it a few kneads. Shape into a rectangle and cut into 8 squares. Arrange the squares on the baking sheet and cook for 20-25 minutes at 360 F on Bake function.

Vanilla Brownies with White Chocolate & Walnuts

Prep + Cook Time: 35 minutes | Serves: 4

Ingredients

6 oz dark chocolate, chopped

6 oz butter

¾ cup white sugar

3 eggs, beaten

2 tsp vanilla extract

¾ cup flour

¼ cup cocoa powder

1 cup chopped walnuts

1 cup white chocolate chips

Directions

Line a baking pan with parchment paper. In a saucepan, melt chocolate and butter over low heat. Do not stop stirring until you obtain a smooth mixture. Let cool slightly and whisk in eggs and vanilla. Sift flour and cocoa and stir to mix well.

Sprinkle the walnuts over and add the white chocolate into the batter. Pour the batter into the pan and cook for 20 minutes in the Cuisinart oven at 350 F on Bake function. Serve chilled with raspberry syrup and ice cream.

Savory Cheddar & Cauliflower Tater Tots

Prep + Cook Time: 35 minutes | Serves: 4

Ingredients

2 lb cauliflower florets, steamed

5 oz cheddar cheese, shredded

1 onion, diced

1 cup breadcrumbs

1 egg, beaten

1 tsp fresh parsley, chopped

1 tsp fresh oregano, chopped

1 tsp fresh chives, chopped

1 tsp garlic powder

Salt and black pepper to taste

Directions

Mash the cauliflower and place it in a large bowl. Add in the onion, parsley, oregano, chives, garlic powder, salt, pepper, and cheddar cheese. Mix with your hands until thoroughly combined and form 12 balls out of the mixture.

Line a baking sheet with parchment paper. Dip half of the tater tots into the egg and then coat with breadcrumbs. Arrange them on the AirFryer Basket and spray with cooking spray.

Fit in the baking sheet and cook in the fryer oven at 390 minutes for 10-12 minutes on Air Fry function. Serve.

Raspberries Maple Pancakes

Prep + Cook Time: 15 minutes | Serves: 4

2 cups all-purpose flour

1 cup milk

3 eggs, beaten

1 tsp baking powder

1 cup brown sugar

1 ½ tsp vanilla extract

½ cup frozen raspberries, thawed

2 tbsp maple syrup

A pinch of salt

Preheat Cuisinart on Bake function to 400 F. In a bowl, mix the flour, baking powder, salt, milk, eggs, vanilla extract, and sugar until smooth. Stir in the raspberries. Do it gently to avoid coloring the batter.

Grease a pie pan with cooking spray. Drop the batter onto the pan. Make sure to leave some space between the pancakes. Cook for 10-15 minutes. Drizzle with maple syrup and serve.

Nutmeg Potato Gratin

Prep + Cook Time: 45 minutes | Serves: 5

5 large potatoes

½ cup sour cream

½ cup grated cheese

½ cup milk

½ tsp nutmeg

Salt and black pepper to taste

Preheat Cuisinart on Bake function to 375 F, peel and slice the potatoes. In a bowl, combine the sour cream, milk, pepper, salt, and nutmeg. Add in the potato slices and stir to coat them well.

Transfer the mixture to an ovenproof casserole. Cook for 15 minutes on Bake function, then sprinkle the cheese on top and cook for 10 minutes. Allow to sit for 10 minutes before serving.

Cheesy Eggs with Fried Potatoes

Prep + Cook Time: 30 minutes | Serves: 4

2 lb potatoes, thinly sliced

1 tbsp olive oil

2 eggs, beaten

2 oz cheddar cheese, grated

1 tbsp all-purpose flour

½ cup coconut cream

Salt and black pepper to taste

Directions

Season the potatoes with salt and pepper and place them in the Cuisinart Air Fryer basket; drizzle with olive oil. Fit in the baking tray and cook for 12 minutes at 350 F on Air Fry function.

Mix the eggs, coconut cream, and flour in a bowl until the cream mixture thickens. Remove the potatoes from the fryer oven, line them in a baking pan and top with the cream mixture. Sprinkle with cheddar cheese. Cook for 12 more minutes. Serve warm.

Crunchy Asparagus with Cheese

Prep + Cook Time: 15 minutes | Serves: 4

Ingredients

1 lb asparagus spears

¼ cup flour

1 cup breadcrumbs

½ cup Parmesan cheese, grated

2 eggs, beaten

Salt and black pepper to taste

Directions

Preheat Cuisinart on Air Fry function to 370 F. Combine the breadcrumbs and Parmesan cheese in a bowl. Season with salt and pepper.

Line a baking sheet with parchment paper. Dip the asparagus spears into the flour first, then into the eggs, and finally coat with crumbs.

Arrange them on the AirFryer Basket, fit in the baking sheet, and cook for about 8 to 10 minutes. Serve with melted butter, hollandaise sauce, or freshly squeezed lemon.

Breaded Cauliflowers in Alfredo Sauce

Prep + Cook Time: 20 minutes | Serves: 4

Ingredients

4 cups cauliflower florets

1 tbsp butter, melted

¼ cup alfredo sauce

1 cup breadcrumbs

1 tsp sea salt

Directions

Whisk the alfredo sauce along with the butter. In a shallow bowl, combine the breadcrumbs with the sea salt. Dip each cauliflower floret into the alfredo mixture first, and then coat in the crumbs. Drop the prepared florets into the Air Fryer basket. Fit in the baking tray.

Set the temperature of your Cuisinart to 380 F and cook for 15 minutes on Air Fry function. Shake the florets twice during cooking. Serve.

Lemon Vanilla Cupcakes with Yogurt Frost

Prep + Cook Time: 25 minutes | Serves: 4

Ingredients

Lemon Frosting:

1 cup natural yogurt

2 tbsp sugar

1 orange, juiced

1 tbsp orange zest

7 oz cream cheese, softened

Cupcake:

2 lemons, seeded and quartered

½ cup flour + extra for basing

¼ tsp salt

2 tbsp sugar

1 tsp baking powder

1 tsp vanilla extract

2 eggs

½ cup butter, softened

2 tbsp milk

Directions

In a bowl, add the yogurt and cream cheese. Mix until smooth. Add in the orange juice and zest; mix well. Gradually add the sugar while stirring until smooth. Make sure the frost is not runny. Set aside.

Place the lemon quarters in a food processor and process it until pureed. Add the flour, baking powder, butter, milk, eggs, vanilla extract, sugar, and salt. Process again until smooth.

Preheat Cuisinart on Bake function to 360 F. Flour the bottom of 8 cupcake cases and spoon the batter into the cases ¾ way up. Place them in the Air Fryer tray and bake for 8-12 minutes. Once ready, remove and let cool. Design the cupcakes with the frosting and serve.

Creamy Vanilla Berry Mini Pies

Prep + Cook Time: 20 minutes | Serves: 4

Ingredients

4 pastry dough sheets

2 tbsp mashed strawberries

2 tbsp mashed raspberries

¼ tsp vanilla extract

2 cups cream cheese, softened

1 tbsp honey

Directions

Preheat fryer on Bake function to 375 F. Divide the cream cheese between the dough sheets and spread it evenly. In a small bowl, combine the berries, honey, and vanilla. Spoon the mixture into the pastry sheets. Pinch the ends of the sheets to form puff. Place the puffs in a lined baking dish. Place the dish in the toaster oven and cook for 15 minutes. Serve chilled.

Olive & Tomato Tart with Feta Cheese

Prep + Cook Time: 25 minutes | Serves: 2

Ingredients

4 eggs

½ cup tomatoes, chopped

1 cup feta cheese, crumbled

1 tbsp fresh basil, chopped

1 tbsp fresh oregano, chopped

¼ cup Kalamata olives, chopped

¼ cup onion, chopped

2 tbsp olive oil

½ cup milk

Salt and black pepper to taste

Preheat Cuisinart on Bake function to 360 F. Brush a pie pan with olive oil. Beat the eggs along with the milk, salt, and pepper. Stir in all of the remaining ingredients. Pour the egg mixture into the pan. Cook for 20 minutes.

Buttery Cheese Sandwich

Prep + Cook Time: 10 minutes | Serves: 1

2 tbsp butter

2 slices bread

3 slices American cheese

Preheat Cuisinart on Bake function to 370 F. Spread one tsp of butter on the outside of each of the bread slices. Place the cheese on the inside of one bread slice. Top with the other slice. Cook in the toaster oven for 4 minutes. Flip the sandwich over and cook for an additional 4 minutes. Serve sliced diagonally.

Creamy Bacon & Egg Wraps with Spicy Salsa

Prep + Cook Time: 15 minutes | Serves: 3

3 tortillas

2 previously scrambled eggs

3 slices bacon, cut into strips

3 tbsp salsa

3 tbsp cream cheese, divided

1 cup grated pepper Jack cheese

Preheat Cuisinart on Air Fry to 390 F. Spread cream cheese onto tortillas. Divide the eggs and bacon between the tortillas. Top with salsa. Sprinkle with cheese. Roll up the tortillas. Place in a greased baking pan and cook for 10 minutes. Serve.

Corn & Chorizo Frittata

Prep + Cook Time: 20 minutes | Serves: 2

4 eggs

1 large potato, boiled and cubed

½ cup frozen corn

½ cup feta cheese, crumbled

1 tbsp fresh parsley, chopped

½ chorizo, sliced

1 tbsp olive oil

Salt and black pepper to taste

Preheat Cuisinart on Air Fry function to 375 F. Heat the olive oil in a skillet over medium heat and cook the chorizo cook for 3 minutes. Beat the eggs with salt and pepper in a bowl. Stir in chorizo and the remaining ingredients. Pour the mixture into the baking pan of Cuisinart oven and cook for 10-15 minutes on Bake function. Serve sliced.

Yogurt & Cream Cheese Zucchini Cakes

Prep + Cook Time: 20 minutes | Serves: 4

Ingredients

1 ½ cups flour

1 tsp cinnamon

3 eggs

2 tsp baking powder

2 tbsp sugar

1 cup milk

2 tbsp butter, melted

1 tbsp yogurt

½ cup shredded zucchini

2 tbsp cream cheese

Directions

In a bowl, whisk the eggs along with the sugar, salt, cinnamon, cream cheese, flour, and baking powder. In another bowl, combine all of the liquid ingredients. Gently combine the dry and liquid mixtures. Stir in zucchini.

Line muffin tins with baking paper, and pour the batter inside them. Arrange on the Air Fryer tray and cook for 15-18 minutes on Bake function at 380 F. Serve chilled.

Prosciutto & Salami Egg Bake

Prep + Cook Time: 20 minutes | Serves: 2

Ingredients

1 beef sausage, chopped

4 slices prosciutto, chopped

3 oz salami, chopped

1 cup grated mozzarella cheese

4 eggs, beaten

½ tsp onion powder

Directions

Preheat Cuisinart on Bake function to 350 F. Whisk the eggs with the onion powder. Brown the sausage in a skillet over medium heat for 2 minutes. Remove to the egg mixture and add in mozzarella cheese, salami, and prosciutto and give it a stir. Pour the egg mixture in a greased baking pan and cook for 10-15 minutes until golden brown on top. Serve.

Almond & Cinnamon Berry Oat Bars

Prep + Cook Time: 40 minutes | Serves: 10

Ingredients

3 cups rolled oats

½ cup ground almonds

½ cup flour

1 tsp baking powder

1 tsp ground cinnamon

3 eggs, lightly beaten

½ cup canola oil

⅓ cup milk

2 tsp vanilla extract

2 cups mixed berries

Directions

Spray the Cuisinart baking pan with cooking spray. In a bowl, add oats, almonds, flour, baking powder and cinnamon into and stir well. In another bowl, whisk eggs, oil, milk, and vanilla.

Stir the wet ingredients gently into the oat mixture. Fold in the berries. Pour the mixture in the pan and place in the toaster oven. Cook for 15-20 minutes at 350 F on Bake function until is nice and soft. Let cool and cut into bars to serve.

Cinnamon Mango Bread

Prep + Cook Time: 60 minutes | Serves: 4

Ingredients

½ cup melted butter

1 egg, lightly beaten

½ cup brown sugar

1 tsp vanilla extract

3 ripe mango, mashed

1 ½ cups plain flour

1 tsp baking powder

½ tsp grated nutmeg

½ tsp ground cinnamon

Directions

Spray the Cuisinart baking pan with cooking spray and line with parchment paper. In a bowl, whisk butter, egg, sugar, vanilla, and mango. Sift in flour, baking powder, nutmeg, and cinnamon and stir without overmixing. Pour the batter into the pan and place in the toaster oven.

Cook for 25-30 minutes at 360 F on Bake function until a toothpick inserted in the middle comes out clean. Let cool on a wire rack before slicing. Serve.

Cheesy Potato & Spinach Frittata

Prep + Cook Time: 35 minutes | Serves: 4

Ingredients

3 cups potato cubes, boiled

2 cups spinach, chopped

5 eggs, lightly beaten

¼ cup heavy cream

1 cup grated mozzarella cheese

½ cup parsley, chopped

Fresh thyme, chopped

Salt and black pepper to taste

Spray the Cuisinart Air Fryer tray with oil. Arrange the potatoes inside.

In a bowl, whisk eggs, cream, spinach, mozzarella, parsley, thyme, salt and pepper, and pour over the potatoes. Cook in your Cuisinart for 16 minutes at 360 F on Bake function until nice and golden. Serve sliced.

Caprese Sandwich with Sourdough Bread

Prep + Cook Time: 15 minutes | Serves: 2

4 slices sourdough bread

2 tbsp mayonnaise

2 slices ham

2 lettuce leaves

1 tomato, sliced

2 slices mozzarella cheese

Salt and black pepper to taste

On a clean board, lay the sourdough slices and spread with mayonnaise. Top 2 of the slices with ham, lettuce, tomato, and mozzarella cheese. Season with salt and pepper.

Top with the remaining two slices to form two sandwiches. Spray with oil and transfer to the Cuisinart Air Fryer basket. Fit in the baking tray and cook for 10 minutes at 350 F on Bake function, flipping once halfway through cooking. Serve hot.

Cheddar Cheese Hash Browns

Prep + Cook Time: 20 minutes | Serves: 4

4 russet potatoes, peeled, grated

1 brown onion, chopped

3 garlic cloves, chopped

½ cup grated cheddar cheese

1 egg, lightly beaten

Salt and black pepper

3 tbsp finely thyme sprigs

In a bowl, mix potatoes, onion, garlic, cheese, egg, salt, black pepper, and thyme. Spray the fryer tray with cooking spray. Press the hash brown mixture into the tray.

Cook in the Cuisinart oven for 12-16 minutes at 400 F on Bake function. Shake once halfway through cooking until the hash browns are golden and crispy. Serve.

Creamy Parmesan & Ham Shirred Eggs

Prep + Cook Time: 20 minutes | Serves: 2

2 tsp butter

4 eggs, divided

2 tbsp heavy cream

4 slices of ham

3 tbsp Parmesan cheese, shredded

¼ tsp paprika

¾ tsp salt

¼ tsp pepper

2 tsp chopped chives

Preheat Cuisinart on Bake function to 320 F. Grease a pie pan with the butter. Arrange the ham slices on the bottom of the pan to cover it completely. Whisk one egg along with the heavy cream, salt, and pepper in a bowl.

Pour the mixture over the ham slices. Crack the other eggs over the ham. Sprinkle with Parmesan cheese. Cook for 14 minutes. Season with paprika, garnish with chives, and serve.

Creamy Mushroom and Spinach Omelet

Prep + Cook Time: 10 minutes | Serves: 2

4 eggs, lightly beaten

2 tbsp heavy cream

2 cups spinach, chopped

1 cup mushrooms, chopped

3 oz feta cheese, crumbled

1 tbsp fresh parsley, chopped

Salt and black pepper to taste

Spray a baking pan with cooking spray. In a bowl, whisk eggs and heavy cream until combined. Stir in spinach, mushrooms, feta, salt, and pepper.

Pour into the basket tray and cook in your Cuisinart for 6-10 minutes at 350 F on Bake function until golden and set. Sprinkle with parsley, cut into wedges, and serve.

Spinach & Kale Balsamic Chicken

Prep + Cook Time: 20 minutes | Serves: 1

½ cup baby spinach leaves

½ cup shredded romaine

3 large kale leaves, chopped

4 oz chicken breasts, cut into cubes

3 tbsp olive oil, divided

1 tsp balsamic vinegar

1 garlic clove, minced

Salt and black pepper to taste

Place the chicken, 1 tbsp of olive oil, and garlic in a bowl. Season with salt and pepper and toss to combine. Put on a lined Air Fryer pan and cook for 14 minutes at 390 F on Bake function.

Place the greens in a large bowl. Add the remaining olive oil and balsamic vinegar. Season with salt and pepper and toss to combine. Top with the chicken and serve.

Tasty Cheddar Omelet

Prep + Cook Time: 20 minutes | Serves: 1

Ingredients

2 eggs

2 tbsp cheddar cheese, grated

1 tsp soy sauce

½ onion, sliced

Salt and black pepper to taste

1 tbsp olive oil

Directions

Preheat Cuisinart on Bake function to 350 F. Whisk the eggs with soy sauce, salt, and pepper. Stir in onion. Grease a baking dish with the olive oil and add in the egg mixture. Cook for 10-14 minutes. Top with the grated cheddar cheese and serve.

Classic Bacon & Egg English Muffin

Prep + Cook Time: 15 minutes | Serves: 1

Ingredients

1 egg

1 English muffin

2 slices of bacon

Salt and black pepper to taste

Directions

Preheat Cuisinart on Bake function to 395 F. Crack the egg into a ramekin. Place the English muffin, egg ramekin, and bacon in a baking pan. Cook for 9 minutes. Let cool slightly so you can assemble the sandwich. Cut the muffin in half. Place the egg on one half and season with salt and pepper. Arrange the bacon on top. Top with the other muffin half.

Salty Parsnip Patties

Prep + Cook Time: 20 minutes | Serves: 2

Ingredients

1 large parsnip, grated

3 eggs, beaten

½ tsp garlic powder

¼ tsp nutmeg

1 tbsp olive oil

1 cup flour

Salt and black pepper to taste

In a bowl, combine flour, eggs, parsnip, nutmeg, and garlic powder. Season with salt and pepper. Form patties out of the mixture. Drizzle the AirFryer basket with olive oil and arrange the patties inside. Fit in the baking tray and cook for 15 minutes on Air Fry function at 360 F. Serve with garlic mayo.

Giant Strawberry Pancake

Prep + Cook Time: 30 minutes | Serves: 3

Ingredients

3 eggs, beaten

2 tbsp butter, melted

½ cup flour

2 tbsp sugar, powdered

½ cup milk

1 ½ cups fresh strawberries, sliced

Directions

Preheat Cuisinart on Bake function to 350 F. In a bowl, mix flour, milk, eggs, and vanilla until fully incorporated. Add the mixture a greased with melted butter pan.

Place the pan in your toaster oven and cook for 12-16 minutes until the pancake is fluffy and golden brown. Drizzle powdered sugar and toss sliced strawberries on top.

Quick Paprika Eggs

Prep + Cook Time: 10 minutes | Serves: 4

Ingredients

4 large eggs

1 tsp paprika

Salt and pepper to taste

¼ cup cottage cheese, crumbled

Directions

Preheat your Cuisinart fryer to 350 F on Bake function. Crack an egg into a muffin cup. Repeat with the remaining cups. Sprinkle with salt and pepper. Top with cottage cheese. Put the cups in the Air Fryer tray and bake for 8-10 minutes. Remove and sprinkle with paprika to serve.

Parsley Onion & Feta Tart

Prep + Cook Time: 30 minutes | Serves: 4

Ingredients

3 ½ pounds Feta cheese

Black pepper to taste

1 whole onion, chopped

2 tbsp parsley, chopped

1 egg yolk

5 sheets frozen filo pastry

Directions

Cut each of the 5 filo sheets into three equal-sized strips. Cover the strips with oil. In a bowl, mix onion, pepper, feta, salt, egg yolk, and parsley.

Make triangles using the cut strips and add a little bit of the feta mixture on top of each triangle. Place the triangles in a greased baking sheet and cook for 5 minutes at 400 F on Bake function. Serve sprinkled with green onions.

Classic Cheddar Cheese Omelet

Prep + Cook Time: 15 minutes | Serves: 1

Ingredients

2 eggs, beaten

Black pepper to taste

1 cup cheddar cheese, shredded

1 whole onion, chopped

2 tbsp soy sauce

Directions

Preheat Cuisinart on Air Fry function to 340 F. In a bowl, mix the eggs with soy sauce, salt, and pepper. Stir in the onion and cheddar cheese.

Pour the egg mixture in a greased baking pan and cook for 10-12 minutes. Serve and enjoy!

Tomato, Basil & Mozzarella Breakfast

Prep + Cook Time: 10 minutes | Serves: 1

Ingredients

2 slices of bread

4 tomato slices

4 mozzarella slices

1 tbsp olive oil

1 tbsp chopped basil

Salt and black pepper to taste

Directions

Preheat Cuisinart on Toast function to 350 F. Place the bread slices in the toaster oven and toast for 5 minutes. Arrange two tomato slices on each bread slice. Season with salt and pepper.

Fresh Kale & Cottage Omelet

Prep + Cook Time: 15 minutes | Serves: 1

Ingredients

3 eggs

3 tbsp cottage cheese

3 tbsp chopped kale

½ tbsp chopped basil

½ tbsp chopped parsley

Salt and black pepper to taste

1 tsp olive oil

Directions

Beat the eggs with salt and pepper in a bowl. Stir in the rest of the ingredients. Drizzle a baking pan with olive oil. Pour in the mixture and place it into the Cuisinart oven. Cook for 10-12 minutes on Bake function at 360 F until slightly golden and set. Serve.

Buttered Apple & Brie Cheese Sandwich

Prep + Cook Time: 10 minutes | Serves: 1

Ingredients

2 bread slices

½ apple, thinly sliced

2 tsp butter

2 oz brie cheese, thinly sliced

Directions

Spread butter on the bread slices. Top with apple slices. Place brie slices on top of the apples. Finish with the other slice of bread. Cook in Cuisinart for 5 minutes at 350 F on Bake function.

Herby Parmesan Bagel

Prep + Cook Time: 10 minutes | Serves: 1

Ingredients

2 tbsp butter, softened

1 tsp dried basil

1 tsp dried parsley

1 tsp garlic powder

1 tbsp Parmesan cheese

Salt and black pepper to taste

1 bagel

Directions

Preheat Cuisinart on Bake function to 370 degrees. Cut the bagel in half. Combine the butter, Parmesan cheese, garlic, basil, and parsley in a small bowl. Season with salt and pepper. Spread the mixture onto the bagel. Place the bagel in a baking pan and cook for 5 minutes. Serve.

Top each slice with 2 mozzarella slices. Return to the oven and cook for 1 minute more. Drizzle the caprese toasts with olive oil and top with chopped basil.

Vanilla & Cinnamon Toast Toppet

Prep + Cook Time: 10 minutes | Serves: 6

Ingredients

12 slices bread

½ cup sugar

1 ½ tsp cinnamon

1 stick of butter, softened

1 tsp vanilla extract

Directions

Preheat Cuisinart on Toast function to 360 F. Combine all ingredients, except the bread, in a bowl. Spread the buttery cinnamon mixture onto the bread slices. Place the bread slices in the toaster oven. Cook for 8 minutes. Serve.

Cinnamon-Orange Toast

Prep + Cook Time: 15 minutes | Serves: 6

12 slices bread

½ cup sugar

1 stick butter

1½ tbsp vanilla extract

1½ tbsp cinnamon

2 oranges, zested

Mix butter, sugar, and vanilla extract and microwave for 30 seconds until everything melts. Add in orange zest. Pour the mixture over bread slices. Lay the bread slices in your Cuisinart Air Fryer pan and cook for 5 minutes at 400 F on Toast function. Serve with berry sauce.

Prosciutto & Mozzarella Crostini

Prep + Cook Time: 7 minutes | Serves: 1

½ cup finely chopped tomatoes

3 oz chopped mozzarella

3 prosciutto slices, chopped

1 tbsp olive oil

1 tsp dried basil

6 small slices of French bread

Preheat Cuisinart on Toast function to 350 F. Place the bread slices in the toaster oven and toast for 5 minutes. Top the bread with tomatoes, prosciutto and mozzarella. Sprinkle the basil over the mozzarella. Drizzle with olive oil. Return to oven and cook for 1 more minute, enough to become melty and warm.

Porridge with Honey & Peanut Butter

Prep + Cook Time: 15 minutes | Serves: 4

2 cups steel-cut oats

1 cup flax seeds

1 tbsp peanut butter

1 tbsp butter

4 cups milk

4 tbsp honey

Preheat Cuisinart on Bake function to 390 F. Combine all of the ingredients in an ovenproof bowl. Place in a baking pan and cook for 7 minutes. Stir and serve.

Peppery Sausage & Parsley Patties

Prep + Cook Time: 20 minutes | Serves: 4

1 lb ground Italian sausage

¼ cup breadcrumbs

1 tsp dried parsley

1 tsp red pepper flakes

½ tsp salt

¼ tsp black pepper

¼ tsp garlic powder

1 egg, beaten

Preheat Cuisinart on Bake function to 350 F. Combine all of the ingredients in a large bowl. Line a baking sheet with parchment paper. Make patties out of the sausage mixture and arrange them on the baking sheet. Cook for 15 minutes, flipping once halfway through cooking. Serve.

Honey Banana Pastry with Berries

Prep + Cook Time: 15 minutes | Serves: 2

Ingredients

3 bananas, sliced

3 tbsp honey

2 puff pastry sheets, cut into thin strips

Fresh berries to serve

Directions

Preheat Cuisinart on Bake function to 340 F. Place the banana slices into a baking dish. Cover with the pastry strips and top with honey. Cook for 12 minutes. Serve with berries.

Appetizers & Side Dishes

Homemade Tortilla Chips

Prep + Cook Time: 55 minutes | Serves: 4

Ingredients

1 cup flour

Salt and black pepper to taste

1 tbsp golden flaxseed meal

2 cups shredded Cheddar cheese

Directions

Melt cheddar cheese in the microwave for 1 minute. Add flour, salt, flaxseed meal, and pepper. Mix well with a fork. On a board, place the dough and knead it with hands while warm until the ingredients are well combined. Divide the dough into 2 and with a rolling pin, roll them out flat into 2 rectangles. Use a pastry cutter to cut out triangle-shaped pieces.

Line them in one layer on the Air Fryer basket and spray with cooking spray. Fit in the baking tray and cook for 10 minutes on Air Fry function at 400 F. Serve with a cheese dip.

Sweet Pickle Chips with Buttermilk

Prep + Cook Time: 20 minutes | Serves: 3

Ingredients

36 sweet pickle chips

1 cup buttermilk

3 tbsp smoked paprika

2 cups flour

¼ cup cornmeal

Salt and black pepper to taste

Directions

Preheat Cuisinart on Air Fryer function to 400 F. In a bowl, mix flour, paprika, pepper, salt, cornmeal, and powder. Place pickles in buttermilk and set aside for 5 minutes. Dip the pickles in the spice mixture and place them in the greased air fryer basket. Fit in the baking tray and cook for 10 minutes. Serve warm.

Grandma's Apple Cinnamon Chips

Prep + Cook Time: 25 minutes | Serves: 2

Ingredients

1 tsp sugar

1 tsp salt

1 whole apple, sliced

½ tsp cinnamon

Confectioners' sugar for serving

Directions

Preheat your Cuisinart to 400 F on Bake function. In a bowl, mix cinnamon, salt, and sugar. Add in the apple slices and toss to coat. Place the prepared apple slices in the greased air fryer basket andfit in the cooking tray. Cook for 10 minutes, flipping once. Dust with sugar and serve.

Crunchy Cheese Twists

Prep + Cook Time: 45 minutes | Serves: 8

Ingredients

2 cups cauliflower florets, steamed

1 egg

3 ½ oz oats

1 red onion, diced

1 tsp mustard

5 oz cheddar cheese, shredded

Salt and black pepper to taste

Directions

Preheat Cuisinart on Air Fry function to 350 F. Place the oats in a food processor and pulse until they are the consistency of breadcrumbs.

Place the cauliflower florets in a large bowl. Add in the rest of the ingredients and mix to combine. Take a little bit of the mixture and twist it into a straw.

Place onto a lined baking tray and repeat the process with the rest of the mixture. Cook for 10 minutes, turn over, and cook for an additional 10 minutes. Serve.

Mixed Nuts with Cinnamon

Prep + Cook Time: 25 minutes | Serves: 4

Ingredients

½ cup pecans

½ cup walnuts

½ cup almonds

A pinch cayenne pepper

2 tbsp sugar

2 tbsp egg whites

2 tsp cinnamon

Directions

Add the pepper, sugar, and cinnamon to a bowl and mix well; set aside. In another bowl, combine the pecans, walnuts, almonds, and egg whites. Add the spice mixture to the nuts and give it a good mix. Lightly grease the baking tray with cooking spray.

Pour in the nuts and cook for 10 minutes on Bake function at 350 F. Shake and cook for further for 10 minutes. Pour the nuts in a bowl. Let cool before serving.

Garlicky Mushroom Spaghetti

Prep + Cook Time: 10 minutes | Serves: 4

Ingredients

½ lb white button mushrooms, sliced

2 tbsp butter, melted

2 garlic cloves, chopped

12 oz spaghetti, cooked

14 oz mushroom sauce (store-bought)

Salt and black pepper to taste

Directions

Preheat Cuisinart on Air Fry function to 400 F. Brush the Air Fryer baking tray with butter and add in mushrooms and garlic. Mix well and cook in the oven for 6-8 minutes. Heat the mushroom sauce in a saucepan over medium heat and stir in the baked mushrooms, 1-2 minutes. Pour the mushroom sauce over the cooked spaghetti and serve.

Cheese Eggplant Boats with Ham & Parsley

Prep + Cook Time: 20 minutes | Serves: 2

Ingredients

1 eggplant

4 ham slices, chopped

1 cup shredded mozzarella cheese

1 tsp dried parsley

Salt and black pepper to taste

Directions

Preheat Cuisinart on Bake function to 330 F. Peel the eggplant and cut it lengthwise in half; scoop some of the flesh out. Season with salt and pepper. Divide half of the mozzarella cheese between the eggplant halves and cover with the ham slices. Top with the remaining mozzarella cheese, sprinkle with parsley, and cook for 12 minutes. Serve warm.

Goat Cheese & Pancetta Bombs

Prep + Cook Time: 25 minutes | Serves: 10

Ingredients

16 oz soft goat cheese

2 tbsp fresh rosemary, finely chopped

1 cup almonds, chopped into small pieces

Salt and black pepper

15 dried plums, chopped

15 pancetta slices

Directions

Line the Cuisinart Air Fryer tray with parchment paper. In a bowl, add goat cheese, rosemary, almonds, salt, pepper, and plums; stir well. Roll into balls and wrap with pancetta slices. Arrange the bombs on the tray and cook for 10 minutes at 400 F. Let cool before serving.

Delicious Chicken Wings with Alfredo Sauce

Prep + Cook Time: 60 minutes | Serves: 4

Ingredients

1 ½ pounds chicken wings

Salt and black pepper to taste

½ cup Alfredo sauce

Directions

Preheat Cuisinart on Air Fry function to 370 F. Season the wings with salt and pepper. Arrange them on the greased basket without touching. Fit in the baking tray and cook for 20 minutes until no longer pink in the center. Work in batches if needed. Increase the heat to 390 F and cook for 5 minutes more. Remove to a large bowl and drizzle with the Alfredo sauce. Serve.

Mini Salmon Quiches

Prep + Cook Time: 20 minutes | Serves: 15

Ingredients

15 mini tart cases

4 eggs, lightly beaten

½ cup heavy cream

Salt and black pepper

3 oz smoked salmon, chopped

6 oz feta cheese, crumbled

2 tsp fresh dill, chopped

Directions

Mix together eggs and heavy cream in a bowl. Arrange the tarts on a greased baking tray. Fill them with the egg mixture, about halfway up the side and top with salmon and feta cheese. Cook for 10 minutes at 360 F on Bake function, regularly checking to avoid overcooking. Sprinkle with dill and serve chilled.

Perfect Crispy Potatoes

Prep + Cook Time: 35 minutes | Serves: 4

Ingredients

1 ½ pounds potatoes, halved

2 tbsp olive oil

3 garlic cloves, grated

1 tbsp minced fresh rosemary

Salt and black pepper to taste

Directions

In a bowl, mix potatoes, olive oil, garlic, rosemary, salt, and pepper until well-coated. Arrange the potatoes on the basket and fit in the baking tray. Cook at 360 F on Air Fry function for 25 minutes, shaking twice until crispy on the outside and tender on the inside. Serve.

Egg Roll Wrapped with Cabbage & Prawns

Prep + Cook Time: 50 minutes | Serves: 4

Ingredients

2 tbsp vegetable oil

1-inch piece fresh ginger, grated

1 tbsp minced garlic

1 carrot, cut into strips

¼ cup chicken broth

2 tbsp reduced-sodium soy sauce

1 tbsp sugar

1 cup shredded Napa cabbage

1 tbsp sesame oil

8 cooked prawns, chopped

1 egg

8 egg roll wrappers

Heat vegetable oil in a skillet over medium heat and sauté ginger and garlic for 40 seconds until fragrant. Stir in carrot and cook for another 2 minutes. Pour in chicken broth, soy sauce, and sugar and bring to a boil. Add in cabbage and let simmer until softened, about 4 minutes. Remove skillet from the heat and stir in sesame oil. Let cool for 15 minutes.

Strain cabbage mixture and fold in prawns. Whisk the egg in a small bowl. Fill each egg roll wrapper with prawn mixture, arranging the mixture just below the center of the wrapper. Fold the bottom part over the filling and tuck under. Fold in both sides and tightly roll-up.

Use the whisked egg to seal the wrapper. Repeat until all egg rolls are ready. Place the rolls into a greased frying basket, spray them with oil and fit in the baking tray. Cook for 12 minutes at 370 F on Air Fry function, turning once halfway through. Serve.

Cheesy Sticks with Thai Sauce

Prep + Cook Time: 20 minutes + freezing time| Serves: 4

Ingredients

12 mozzarella string cheese

2 cups breadcrumbs

3 eggs

1 cup sweet Thai sauce

4 tbsp skimmed milk

Directions

Pour the crumbs in a bowl. Crack the eggs into another bowl and beat with the milk. One after the other, dip each cheese sticks in the egg mixture, in the crumbs, then egg mixture again and then in the crumbs back. Place the cheese sticks in a cookie sheet and freeze for 2 hours.

Preheat Cuisinart on Air Fry function to 380 F. Arrange the sticks in the frying basket without overcrowding. Fit in the baking tray and cook for 8 minutes, flipping them halfway through cooking until browned. Serve with the Thai sauce.

Jalapeno Popper Chicken with Bacon

Prep + Cook Time: 40 minutes | Serves: 4

Ingredients

8 Jalapeno peppers, halved and seeded

4 chicken breasts, butterflied and halved

6 oz cream cheese

6 oz Cheddar cheese

16 slices bacon

1 cup breadcrumbs

Salt and black pepper to taste

2 eggs

Directions

Season the chicken with salt and pepper. In a bowl, add cream and cheddar cheeses and mix well. Take each jalapeno and spoon in the cheese mixture to the brim. On a working board, flatten each piece of chicken and lay 2 bacon slices each on them. Place a stuffed jalapeno on each laid out chicken and bacon set, and wrap the peppers in them.

Preheat Cuisinart on Air Fry function to 350 F. Add the eggs to a bowl and pour the breadcrumbs in another bowl. Take each wrapped jalapeno and dip it into the eggs and then in the breadcrumbs.

Working in batches, arrange the breaded peppers in the greased fryer basket, fit in the baking tray, and cook for 7 minutes. Turn the jalapenos and cook further for 4 minutes.

Once ready, remove them onto a paper towel-lined plate. Repeat the cooking process for the remaining jalapenos. Serve with a sweet dip for an enhanced taste.

Maple Shrimp with Coconut

Prep + Cook Time: 30 minutes | Serves: 3

Ingredients

1 lb jumbo shrimp, peeled and deveined

¾ cup shredded coconut

1 tbsp maple syrup

½ cup breadcrumbs

⅓ cup cornstarch

½ cup milk

Directions

Pour the cornstarch in a zipper bag, add shrimp, zip the bag up and shake vigorously to coat with the cornstarch. Mix the syrup and milk in a bowl and set aside.

In a separate bowl, mix the breadcrumbs and shredded coconut. Open the zipper bag and remove each shrimp while shaking off excess starch. Dip shrimp in the milk mixture and then in the crumb mixture while pressing loosely to trap enough crumbs and coconut.

Place in the basket without overcrowding and fit in the baking tray. Cook for 12 minutes at 350 F on Air Fry function, flipping once halfway through until golden brown. Serve warm.

Sesame Garlic Chicken Wings

Prep + Cook Time: 55 minutes | Serves: 4

Ingredients

1 pound chicken wings

1 cup soy sauce, divided

½ cup brown sugar

½ cup apple cider vinegar

2 tbsp fresh ginger, minced

2 tbsp fresh garlic, minced

1 tsp finely ground black pepper

2 tbsp cornstarch

2 tbsp cold water

1 tsp sesame seeds

Directions

In a bowl, mix the chicken wings with a half cup of the soy sauce. Refrigerate for 20 minutes; drain and pat dry. Arrange the wings on the Air Fryer basket and fit in the baking tray. Cook for 20 minutes at 380 F on Air Fry function, turning once halfway through.

In a skillet over medium heat, stir sugar, remaining soy sauce, vinegar, ginger, garlic, and pepper. Cook until sauce has reduced slightly. Dissolve cornstarch in cold water and stir in the sauce; cook until it thickens, 2 minutes. Pour the sauce over wings and sprinkle with sesame seeds.

Whole Chicken with BBQ Sauce

Prep + Cook Time: 25 minutes | Serves: 3

Ingredients

1 whole small chicken, cut into pieces

1 tsp salt

1 tsp smoked paprika

1 tsp garlic powder

1 cup BBQ sauce

Directions

Coat the chicken with salt, paprika, and garlic. Place the chicken pieces skin-side down in the greased baking tray. Cook in the Cuisinart oven for around 15 minutes at 400 F on Bake function until slightly golden. Remove to a plate and brush with barbecue sauce. Return the chicken to the oven skin-side up and cook for 5 minutes at 340 F. Serve with more barbecue sauce.

Cheesy Crisps

Prep + Cook Time: 25 minutes | Serves: 3

Ingredients

4 tbsp grated cheddar cheese + extra for rolling

1 cup flour + extra for kneading

¼ tsp chili powder

½ tsp baking powder

3 tsp butter

A pinch of salt

Directions

In a bowl, add the cheddar cheese, flour, baking powder, chili powder, butter, and salt and mix until the mixture becomes crusty. Add some drops of water and mix well to get a dough. Remove the dough on a flat surface.

Rub some extra flour in your palms and on the surface and knead the dough for a while. Using a rolling pin, roll the dough out into a thin sheet. With a pastry cutter, cut the dough into your desired lings' shape. Add the cheese lings to the greased baking tray and cook for 8 minutes at 350 F on Air Fry function, flipping once halfway through. Serve.

Allspice Chicken Wings

Prep + Cook Time: 45 minutes | Serves: 4

Ingredients

½ tsp celery salt

½ tsp bay leaf powder

½ tsp ground black pepper

½ tsp paprika

¼ tsp dry mustard

¼ tsp cayenne pepper

¼ tsp allspice

2 pounds chicken wings

Directions

Preheat your Cuisinart to 340 F on Air Fry function. In a bowl, mix celery salt, bay leaf powder, black pepper, paprika, dry mustard, cayenne pepper, and allspice. Coat the wings thoroughly in this mixture.

Arrange the wings in an even layer in the greased frying basket and fit in the baking tray. Cook the chicken until it's no longer pink around the bone, about 20 minutes. Then, increase the temperature to 380 F and cook for 6 minutes more until crispy on the outside. Serve warm.

Pineapple Pork Ribs

Prep + Cook Time: 30 minutes | Serves: 4

Ingredients

2 lb cut spareribs

7 oz salad dressing

1 (5-oz) can pineapple juice

2 cups water

Salt and black pepper to taste

Directions

Preheat your Cuisinart to 390 F on Bake function. Sprinkle the ribs with salt and pepper and place them in a greased baking dish. Cook for 15 minutes. Prepare the sauce by combining the salad dressing and the pineapple juice. Serve the ribs drizzled with the sauce.

Parsley Mushroom Pilaf

Prep + Cook Time: 40 minutes | Serves: 6

Ingredients

3 tbsp olive oil

4 cups heated vegetable stock

2 cups long-grain rice

1 onion, chopped

2 garlic cloves, minced

2 cups cremini mushrooms, chopped

Salt and black pepper to taste

1 tbsp fresh chopped parsley, or to taste

Directions

Preheat Cuisinart on Bake function to 400 F. Heat olive oil in a frying pan over medium heat. Add in mushrooms, onion, and garlic and cook for 5 minutes until tender. Stir in the rice for 1 minute and pour in the stock. Season with salt and pepper.

Transfer to your Air Fryer baking dish and cook for 20 minutes. Serve sprinkled with fresh chopped parsley.

Savory Chicken Nuggets with Parmesan Cheese

Prep + Cook Time: 25 minutes | Serves: 4

Ingredients

1 lb chicken breasts, cubed

Salt and black pepper to taste

2 tbsp olive oil

5 tbsp plain breadcrumbs

2 tbsp panko breadcrumbs

2 tbsp grated Parmesan cheese

Preheat Cuisinart on Air Fry function to 380 F. Season the chicken with salt and pepper; set aside. In a bowl, mix the breadcrumbs with the Parmesan cheese.

Brush the chicken pieces with the olive oil, then dip into breadcrumb mixture, and transfer to the Air Fryer basket. Fit in the baking tray and lightly spray chicken with cooking spray. Cook for 10 minutes, flipping once halfway through until golden brown on the outside and no more pink on the inside. Serve warm.

Dill Pickles with Parmesan

Prep + Cook Time: 35 minutes | Serves: 4

Ingredients

3 cups dill pickles, sliced, drained

2 eggs

2 tsp water

1 cup grated Parmesan cheese

1 ½ cups breadcrumbs, smooth

Black pepper to taste

Directions

Preheat Cuisinart on Air Fry function to 400 F. In a bowl, add the breadcrumbs and black pepper and mix well. In another bowl, crack the eggs and beat with the water. Add the Parmesan cheese to a separate bowl.

Pull out the fryer basket and spray it lightly with cooking spray. Dredge the pickle slices it in the egg mixture, then in breadcrumbs and then in cheese. Place them in the basket without overlapping and fit in the baking tray. Cook for 4 minutes. Turn them and cook for further for 5 minutes until crispy. Serve with cheese dip.

Grandma's Chicken Thighs

Prep + Cook Time: 30 minutes | Serves: 2

Ingredients

1 pound chicken thighs

½ tsp salt

¼ tsp black pepper

¼ tsp garlic powder

Directions

Season the thighs with salt, pepper, and garlic powder. Arrange thighs, skin side down, on the Cuisinart Air Fryer basket and fit in the baking tray. Cook until golden brown, about 20 minutes at 350 F on Bake function. Serve immediately.

Homemade Cod Fingers

Prep + Cook Time: 25 minutes | Serves: 3

Ingredients

2 cups flour

Salt and black pepper to taste

1 tsp seafood seasoning

2 whole eggs, beaten

1 cup cornmeal

1 pound cod fillets, cut into fingers

2 tbsp milk

2 eggs, beaten

1 cup breadcrumbs

1 lemon, cut into wedges

Preheat Cuisinart on Air Fryer function to 400 F. In a bowl, mix beaten eggs with milk. In a separate bowl, combine flour, cornmeal, and seafood seasoning. In another mixing bowl, mix spices with the eggs. In a third bowl, pour the breadcrumbs.

Dip cod fingers in the seasoned flour mixture, followed by a dip in the egg mixture, and finally coat with breadcrumbs. Place the fingers in your Air Fryer basket and fit in the baking tray. Cook for 10 minutes until golden brown. Serve with lemon wedges.

Stuffed Mushrooms with Rice & Cheese

Prep + Cook Time: 30 minutes | Serves: 10

Ingredients

10 Swiss brown mushrooms

2 tbsp olive oil

1 cup cooked brown rice

1 cup grated Grana Padano cheese

1 tsp dried mixed herbs

Salt and black pepper to taste

Directions

Brush mushrooms with oil and arrange onto the Cuisinart Air Fryer baking tray. In a bowl, mix rice, Grana Padano cheese, herbs, salt, and pepper. Stuff the mushrooms with the mixture. Cook in the oven for 14 minutes at 360 F on Bake function until the cheese has melted. Serve.

Party Chicken Wings

Prep + Cook Time: 20 minutes | Serves: 3

Ingredients

15 chicken wings

Salt and black pepper to taste

⅓ cup chili sauce

⅓ cup butter

½ tbsp vinegar

Directions

Preheat Cuisinart on Air Fry function to 360 F. Season the wings with salt and pepper. Add them to the greased basket and fit in the baking tray. Cook for 15 minutes. Toss every 5 minutes. Once ready, remove them to a bowl.

Melt the butter in a saucepan over low heat. Add in the vinegar and hot sauce. Stir and cook for a minute. Turn the heat off. Pour the sauce over the chicken. Toss to coat thoroughly. Transfer the chicken to a serving platter. Serve with a side of celery strips and blue cheese dressing.

Creamy Eggplant Cakes

Prep + Cook Time: 20 minutes | Serves: 4

1 ½ cups flour

1 tsp cinnamon

3 eggs

2 tsp baking powder

2 tbsp sugar

1 cup milk

2 tbsp butter, melted

1 tbsp yogurt

½ cup shredded eggplant

Pinch of salt

2 tbsp cream cheese

Preheat Cuisinart on Air Fry function to 350 F. In a bowl, whisk the eggs along with the sugar, salt, cinnamon, cream cheese, flour, and baking powder. In another bowl, combine all of the liquid ingredients. Gently combine the dry and liquid mixtures; stir in eggplant.

Line the muffin tins and pour the batter inside; cook for 12 minutes. Check with a toothpick: you may need to cook them for an additional 2 to 3 minutes. Serve chilled.

Thyme & Carrot Cookies

Prep + Cook Time: 30 minutes | Serves: 8

6 carrots, sliced

Salt and black pepper to taste

1 tbsp parsley

1 ¼ oz oats

1 whole egg, beaten

1 tbsp thyme

Preheat Cuisinart on Air Fryer function to 360 F. In a saucepan, add carrots and cover with hot water. Cook over medium heat for 10 minutes until tender. Remove to a plate. Season with salt, pepper, and parsley and mash using a fork. Add the beaten egg, oats, and thyme as you continue mashing to mix well.

Form the batter into cookie shapes. Place in your Air Fryer baking tray and cook for 15 minutes until edges are browned. Serve chilled.

Garlic Lemon Roasted Chicken

Prep + Cook Time: 60 minutes | Serves: 4

1 (3 ½ pounds) whole chicken

2 tbsp olive oil

Salt and black pepper to taste

1 lemon, cut into quarters

5 garlic cloves

Preheat Cuisinart on Air Fry function to 360 F. Brush the chicken with olive oil and season with salt and pepper. Stuff with lemon and garlic cloves into the cavity.

Place the chicken breast-side down onto the Cuisinart Air Fryer basket. Tuck the legs and wings tips under. Fit in the baking tray and cook for 45 minutes at 350 F on Bake function. Let rest for 5-6 minutes, then carve and serve.

Chickpeas with Rosemary & Sage

Prep + Cook Time: 20 minutes | Serves: 4

Ingredients

2 (14.5-ounce) cans chickpeas, rinsed

2 tbsp olive oil

1 tsp dried rosemary

½ tsp dried thyme

¼ tsp dried sage

¼ tsp salt

Directions

In a bowl, mix together chickpeas, oil, rosemary, thyme, sage, and salt. Transfer them to the Cuisinart Air Fryer baking dish and spread in an even layer. Cook for 15 minutes at 380 F on Bake function, shaking once halfway through cooking. Serve.

Crispy Onion Rings with Buttermilk

Prep + Cook Time: 30 minutes | Serves: 4

Ingredients

2 sweet onions

2 cups buttermilk

2 cups pancake mix

2 cups water

1 package cornbread mix

1 tsp salt

Directions

Preheat Cuisinart on Air Fry function to 370 F. Slice the onions into rings. Combine the pancake mix with water. Line a baking sheet with parchment paper. Dip the rings in the cornbread mixture first, and then in the pancake batter.

Place the onion rings onto the greased basket and then into the baking tray. Cook for 8-12 minutes, flipping once until crispy. Serve with salsa rosa.

Easy Crunchy Garlic Croutons

Prep + Cook Time: 20 minutes | Serves: 4

Ingredients

2 cups bread, cubed

2 tbsp butter, melted

Garlic salt and black pepper to taste

In a bowl, toss the bread cubes with butter, garlic salt, and pepper until well-coated. Place the cubes in the Air Fryer basket and fit in the baking tray. Cook in the Cuisinart oven for 12 minutes at 380 F on Air Fry function or until golden brown and crispy.

Traditional French Fries

Prep + Cook Time: 30 minutes | Serves: 2

Ingredients

2 russet potatoes, cut into strips

2 tbsp olive oil

Salt and black pepper to taste

Directions

Spray the Cuisinart Air Fryer basket with cooking spray. In a bowl, toss the strips with olive oil until well-coated and season with salt and pepper.

Arrange on the Air Fryer basket and fit in the baking tray. Cook for 20-25 minutes at 400 F on Air Fry function, turning once halfway through. Check for crispiness and serve immediately with garlic aioli, ketchup, or crumbled cheese.

Gourmet Beef Sticks

Prep + Cook Time: 10 minutes + chilling time| Serves: 3

Ingredients

1 lb ground beef

3 tbsp sugar

A pinch garlic powder

A pinch chili powder

Salt to taste

1 tsp liquid smoke

Directions

Place the beef, sugar, garlic powder, chili powder, salt and liquid smoke in a bowl. Mix well. Mold out 4 sticks with your hands, place them on a plate, and refrigerate for 30 minutes.

Remove and cook in the Cuisinart oven at 350 F for 10 minutes on Bake function. Flip and continue cooking for another 5 minutes until browned.

Simple Chicken Breasts

Prep + Cook Time: 30 minutes | Serves: 4

Ingredients

4 boneless, skinless chicken breasts

1 tsp salt and black pepper

1 tsp garlic powder

Directions

Spray the breasts and the Cuisinart Air Fryer basket with cooking spray. Rub chicken with salt, garlic powder, and black pepper. Arrange the breasts on the basket. Fit in the baking pan and cook for 20 minutes at 360 F on Bake function until nice and crispy. Serve warm.

Cabbage Wedges with Parmesan

Prep + Cook Time: 30 minutes | Serves: 4

½ head of cabbage, cut into 4 wedges

4 tbsp butter, melted

2 cups Parmesan cheese, grated

Salt and black pepper to taste

1 tsp smoked paprika

Preheat Cuisinart on Air Fry function to 330 F. Line a baking sheet with parchment paper. Brush the cabbage wedges with the butter. Season with salt and pepper.

Coat cabbage with Parmesan cheese and arrange on the baking pan; sprinkle with paprika. Cook for 15 minutes, flip, and cook for an additional 10 minutes. Serve with yogurt dip.

Crispy Calamari Rings

Prep + Cook Time: 10 minutes + chilling time| Serves: 4

1 lb calamari (squid), cut in rings

¼ cup flour

2 large beaten eggs

1 cup breadcrumbs

Coat the calamari rings with the flour and dip them in the eggs. Then, dip in the breadcrumbs. Refrigerate for 30 minutes. Remove and arrange on the Air Fryer basket and apply cooking spray. Fit in the baking tray and cook for 9 minutes at 380 F on Air Fry function. Serve with garlic mayo and lemon wedges.

Homemade Cheesy Sticks

Prep + Cook Time: 5 minutes | Serves: 12

6 (6 oz) bread cheese

2 tbsp butter

2 cups panko crumbs

Put the butter in a bowl and melt in the microwave for 2 minutes; set aside. With a knife, cut the cheese into equal-sized sticks. Brush each stick with butter and dip into panko crumbs. Arrange the sticks in a single layer in the basket. Fit in the baking tray and cook in the Cuisinart at 390 F for 10 minutes on Air Fry function. Flip halfway through. Serve warm.

Party Macaroni Quiche with Greek Yogurt

Prep + Cook Time: 30 minutes | Serves: 4

8 tbsp leftover macaroni with cheese

Extra cheese for serving

Pastry as much needed for forming 4 shells

Salt and black pepper to taste

1 tsp garlic puree

2 tbsp Greek yogurt

2 whole eggs

12 oz milk

Directions

Preheat Cuisinart on Air Fry function to 360 F. Roll the pastry to form 4 shells. Place them in the Air Fryer pan.

In a bowl, mix leftover macaroni with cheese, yogurt, eggs, milk, and garlic puree. Spoon this mixture into the pastry shells. Top with the cheese evenly. Cook for 20 minutes.

Feta Lime Corn

Prep + Cook Time: 20 minutes | Serves: 2

Ingredients

2 ears of corn

Juice of 2 small limes

2 tsp paprika

4 oz feta cheese, grated

Directions

Preheat Cuisinart on Air Fry function to 370 F. Peel the corn and remove the silk. Place the corn in the baking pan and cook for 15 minutes. Squeeze the juice of 1 lime on top of each ear of corn. Top with feta cheese and serve.

Bacon & Potato Salad with Mayonnaise

Prep + Cook Time: 10 minutes | Serves: 6

Ingredients:

4 lb boiled and cubed potatoes

15 bacon slices, chopped

2 cups shredded cheddar cheese

15 oz sour cream

2 tbsp mayonnaise

1 tsp salt

1 tsp pepper

1 tsp dried herbs, any

Directions

Preheat Cuisinart on Air Fry function to 350 F. Combine the potatoes, bacon, salt, pepper, and herbs in a large bowl. Transfer to the Cuisinart baking pan. Cook for about 7 minutes. Remove and stir in sour cream and mayonnaise and serve.

Garlic Potato Chips

Prep + Cook Time: 30 minutes + marinating time| Serves: 3

Ingredients

3 whole potatoes, cut into thin slices

¼ cup olive oil

1 tbsp garlic

½ cup cream

2 tbsp rosemary

Preheat Cuisinart on Air Fry function to 390 F. In a bowl, add oil, garlic, and salt to form a marinade. Stir in the potatoes. Allow sitting for 30 minutes.

Lay the potato slices onto the Air Fryer basket and fit in the baking tray. Cook for 20 minutes. After 10 minutes, give the chips a turn. When readt, sprinkle with rosemary and serve.

Spicy Pumpkin-Ham Fritters

Prep + Cook Time: 10 minutes | Serves: 4

Ingredients

1 oz ham, chopped

1 cup dry pancake mix

1 egg

2 tbsp canned puree pumpkin

1 oz cheddar, shredded

½ tsp chili powder

3 tbsp of flour

1 oz beer

2 tbsp scallions, chopped

Directions

Preheat Cuisinart on Air Fry function to 370 F. In a bowl, combine the pancake mix and chili powder. Mix in the egg, puree pumpkin, beer, shredded cheddar, ham and scallions. Form balls and roll them in the flour.

Arrange the balls into the basket and fit in the baking tray. Cook for 8 minutes. Drain on paper towel before serving.

Holiday Pumpkin Wedges

Prep + Cook Time: 30 minutes | Serves: 3

Ingredients

½ pumpkin, washed and cut into wedges

1 tbsp paprika

1 whole lime, squeezed

1 cup paleo dressing

1 tbsp balsamic vinegar

Salt and black pepper to taste

1 tsp turmeric

Directions

Preheat Cuisinart on Air Fry function to 360 F. Place the pumpkin wedges in your Air Fryer baking tray and cook for 20 minutes. In a bowl, mix lime juice, vinegar, turmeric, salt, pepper and paprika to form a marinade. Pour the marinade over pumpkin and cook for 5 more minutes.

Savory Parsley Crab Cakes

Prep + Cook Time: 20 minutes | Serves: 6

1 lb crab meat, shredded

2 eggs, beaten

½ cup breadcrumbs

⅓ cup finely chopped green onion

¼ cup parsley, chopped

1 tbsp mayonnaise

1 tsp sweet chili sauce

½ tsp paprika

Salt and black pepper to taste

In a bowl, add crab meat, eggs, crumbs, green onion, parsley, mayo, chili sauce, paprika, salt and black pepper; mix well with your hands.

Shape into 6 cakes and grease them lightly with oil. Arrange them in the fryer basket without overcrowding. Fit in the baking tray and cook for 8 minutes at 400 F on Air Fry function, turning once halfway through.

Ham Rolls with Vegetables & Walnuts

Prep + Cook Time: 15 minutes | Serves: 4

8 ham slices

4 carrots, chopped

4 slices ham

2 oz walnuts, finely chopped

1 zucchini

1 clove garlic

1 tbsp olive oil

1 tbsp ginger powder

¼ cup basil leaves, finely chopped

Salt and black pepper to taste

Heat the olive oil in a pan over medium heat and add the zucchini, carrots, garlic, ginger and salt; cook for 5 minutes. Add the basil and walnuts, and keep stirring.

Divide the mixture between the ham slices. Then fold one side above the filling and roll in. Cook the rolls in the preheated Cuisinart for 8 minutes at 300 F on Bake function.

Potato Chips with Lemony Dip

Prep + Cook Time: 25 minutes | Serves: 3

3 large potatoes, sliced

1 cup sour cream

2 scallions, white part minced

3 tbsp olive oil.

½ tsp lemon juice

salt and black pepper

Preheat Cuisinart on Air Fry function to 350 F. Place the potatoes into the AirFryer basket Cuisinart and fit in the baking tray. Cook for 15 minutes, flipping once. Season with salt and pepper. Mix sour cream, olive oil, scallions, lemon juice, salt, and pepper and serve with chips.

Bok Choy Crisps

Prep + Cook Time: 10 minutes | Serves: 2

Ingredients

2 tbsp olive oil

4 cups packed bok choy

1 tsp vegan seasoning

1 tbsp yeast flakes

Sea salt, to taste

Directions

In a bowl, mix oil, bok choy, yeast, and vegan seasoning. Dump the coated kale in the Air fryer basket. Set the temperature of your Cuisinart toaster oven to 360 F on Air Fry function and cook for 5 minutes. Shake after 3 minutes. Serve sprinkled with sea salt.

Amul Cheesy Cabbage Canapes

Prep + Cook Time: 15 minutes | Serves: 2

Ingredients

1 whole cabbage, washed and cut in rounds

1 cube Amul cheese

½ carrot, cubed

¼ onion, cubed

¼ red bell pepper, cubed

1 tsp fresh basil, chopped

Directions

Preheat Cuisinart on Air Fry function to 360 F. Using a bowl, mix onion, carrot, bell pepper, and cheese. Toss to coat everything evenly. Add cabbage rounds to the Air fryer baking pan.

Top with the veggie mixture and cook for 8 minutes. Garnish with basil and serve.

Feta Butterbeans with Crispy Bacon

Prep + Cook Time: 10 minutes | Serves: 2

Ingredients

1 (14 oz) can butter beans

1 tbsp chives

3 ½ oz feta, crumbled

Black pepper to taste

1 tsp olive oil

3 ½ oz bacon, sliced

Preheat Cuisinart on Air Fry function to 340 F. Blend beans, olive oil, and pepper in a blender. Arrange bacon slices on your Air fryer basket. Sprinkle chives on top and fit in the baking pan. Cook for 12 minutes. Add feta cheese to the bean mixture and stir. Serve bacon with the dip.

French Beans with Toasted Almonds

Prep + Cook Time: 25 minutes | Serves: 4

Ingredients

1 ½ lb French beans, trimmed

Salt and black pepper to taste

½ pound shallots, chopped

3 tbsp olive oil

½ cup almonds, toasted

Directions

Preheat Cuisinart on Air Fry function to 400 F. Blanch the French beans in filled with water pot over medium heat until tender, about 5-6 minutes. Remove with slotted spoon toa bowl and mix in olive oil, shallots, salt, and pepper. Add the mixture to a baking dish and cook in your Cuisinart for 10 minutes, shaking once or twice. Serve sprinkled with almonds.

Shrimp with Spices

Prep + Cook Time: 15 minutes | Serves: 3

Ingredients

½ pound shrimp, deveined

½ tsp Cajun seasoning

Salt and black pepper to taste

1 tbsp olive oil

¼ tsp paprika

Directions

Preheat Cuisinart on Air Fry function to 390 F. In a bowl, mix paprika, salt, pepper, olive oil, and Cajun seasoning. Add in the shrimp and toss to coat. Transfer the prepared shrimp to the AirFryer basket and fit in the baking tray. Cook for 10-12 minutes, flipping halfway through.

Bacon Wrapped Asparagus

Serves: 4 | Prep + Cook Time: 25 minutes | Serves: 4

Ingredients

20 spears asparagus

4 bacon slices

1 tbsp olive oil

1 tbsp sesame oil

1 tbsp brown sugar

1 garlic clove, crushed

Directions

Preheat Cuisinart on Air Fry function to 380 F. In a bowl, mix the oils, sugar, and crushed garlic. Separate the asparagus into 4 bunches (5 spears in 1 bunch) and wrap each bunch with a bacon slice.

Coat the bunches with the oil mixture. Place them in your Air Fryer basket and fit in the baking tray. Cook for 8 minutes, shaling once. Serve warm.

Brussels Sprouts with Garlic

Prep + Cook Time: 25 minutes | Serves: 2

1 lb Brussels sprouts, trimmed

½ tsp garlic, chopped

2 tbsp olive oil

Salt and black pepper to taste

In a bowl, mix olive oil, garlic, salt, and pepper. Stir in the Brussels sprouts and let rest for 5 minutes. Place the coated sprouts in the Cuisinart Air Fryer basket and fit in the baking tray. Cook for 15 minutes at 380 F, shaking once. Serve warm.

Yogurt Masala Cashew

Prep + Cook Time: 25 minutes | Serves: 2

Ingredients

8 oz Greek yogurt

2 tbsp mango powder

8¾ oz cashew nuts

Salt and black pepper to taste

1 tsp coriander powder

½ tsp masala powder

½ tsp black pepper powder

Directions

Preheat Cuisinart on Air Fry function to 350 F. In a bowl, mix all powders, salt, and pepper. Add in cashews and toss to coat thoroughly. Place the cashews in your Air Fryer baking pan and cook for 15 minutes, shaking every 5 minutes. Serve.

Simple Parmesan Sandwich

Prep + Cook Time: 20 minutes | Serves: 1

Ingredients

2 tbsp Parmesan cheese, shredded

2 scallions, chopped

2 tbsp butter

2 slices bread

¾ cup cheddar cheese

Directions

Preheat Cuisinart on Air Fry function to 360 F. Lay the bread slices on a flat surface. On one slice, spread the exposed side with butter, followed by cheddar and scallions. On the other slice, spread butter and then sprinkle with the Parmesan cheese.

Bring the buttered sides together to form sandwich. Place it in the cooking basket and cook for 10 minutes. Serve with berry sauce.

Savory Curly Potatoes

Prep + Cook Time: 20 minutes | Serves: 2

Ingredients

2 potatoes, spiralized

1 tbsp extra-virgin olive oil

Salt and black pepper to taste

1 tsp paprika

Directions

Preheat Cuisinart on Air Fry function to 350 F. Place the potatoes in a bowl and coat with oil. Transfer them to the cooking basket and fit in the baking tray. Cook for 15 minutes, shaking once. Sprinkle with salt, pepper, and paprika and to serve.

Tasty Carrot Chips

Prep + Cook Time: 20 minutes | Serves: 2

Ingredients

3 large carrots, washed and peeled

Salt to taste

Directions

Using a mandolin slicer, slice the carrots very thinly heightwise. Put the carrot strips in a bowl and season with salt. Grease the fryer basket lightly with cooking spray, and add the carrot strips. Fit in the baking tray and cook in the Cuisinart at 350 F for 10 minutes on Air Fry function, stirring once halfway through. Serve warm.

French-Style Fries

Prep + Cook Time: 35 minutes | Serves: 4

Ingredients

4 russet potatoes, cut into 3-inch pieces

2 tbsp olive oil

Salt and black pepper to taste

Directions

Preheat Cuisinart on Air Fry function to 360 F. Drizzle the potatoes with olive oil and toss to coat. Place the potatoes in the Air Fryer basket and fit in the baking tray. Cook for 20-25 minutes. Sprinkle with salt and pepper and to serve.

Cheese & Chive Scones

Serves: 10 | Prep + Cook Time: 25 minutes | Serves: 10

Ingredients

1 cup flour

Salt and black pepper to taste

¾ oz butter, softened

1 tsp fresh chives, chopped

1 whole egg

1 tbsp milk

1 cup cheddar cheese, shredded

Preheat Cuisinart on Air Fry function to 340 F. In a bowl, mix butter, flour, cheddar cheese, chives, milk, and egg to get a sticky dough. Dust a flat surface with flour. Roll the dough into small balls. Place the balls in the baking pan and cook for 20 minutes. Serve and enjoy!

Pineapple & Mozzarella Tortillas

Prep + Cook Time: 15 minutes | Serves: 2

Ingredients

2 tortillas

8 ham slices

8 mozzarella slices

8 thin pineapple slices

2 tbsp tomato sauce

½ tsp dried parsley

Directions

Preheat Cuisinart on Air Fry function to 330 F. Spread the tomato sauce onto the tortillas. Arrange 4 ham slices on each tortilla. Top the ham with the pineapple and sprinkle with mozzarella and parsley. Cook for 10 minutes and enjoy.

Marinara Chicken Breasts

Prep + Cook Time: 20 minutes | Serves: 2

Ingredients

2 chicken breasts, ½ inch thick

1 egg, beaten

½ cup breadcrumbs

A pinch of salt and black pepper

2 tbsp marinara sauce

2 tbsp Grana Padano cheese, grated

2 slices mozzarella cheese

Directions

Dip the breasts into the egg, then into the crumbs, and arrange on the Air fryer baking sheet. Cook for 6-8 minutes at 400 F on Air Fry function. Turn over and drizzle with marinara sauce, Grana Padano and mozzarella cheeses. Cook for 5 more minutes. Serve.

Easy Parsnip Fries

Prep + Cook Time: 15 minutes | Serves: 3

Ingredients

4 parsnips, sliced

¼ cup flour

¼ cup olive oil

¼ cup water

A pinch of salt

Directions

Preheat Cuisinart on Air Fry function to 390 F. In a bowl, add the flour, olive oil, water, and parsnips; mix to coat. Line the fries in the greased Air Fryer basket and fit in the baking tray. Cook for 15 minutes. Serve with yogurt and garlic dip.

Air Fried Mac & Cheese

Prep + Cook Time: 15 minutes | Serves: 1

Ingredients

1 cup cooked macaroni

1 cup grated cheddar cheese

½ cup warm milk

1 tbsp Parmesan cheese

Salt and black pepper to taste

Directions

Preheat Cuisinart on Air Fry function to 350 F. Add the macaroni to Air Fryer baking pan. Stir in the cheddar cheese and milk. Season with salt and pepper. Place the dish in the toaster oven and cook for 10 minutes. Sprinkle with Parmesan cheese and serve.

Homemade Cheddar Biscuits

Prep + Cook Time: 35 minutes | Serves: 8

Ingredients

½ cup + 1 tbsp butter

2 tbsp sugar

3 cups flour

1 ⅓ cups buttermilk

½ cup cheddar cheese, grated

Directions

Preheat Cuisinart on Bake function to 380 F. Lay a parchment paper on a baking plate. In a bowl, mix sugar, flour, ½ cup of butter, half of the cheddar cheese, and buttermilk to form a batter. Make 8 balls from the batter and roll in flour.

Place the balls in your Air Fryer baking tray and flatten into biscuit shapes. Sprinkle the remaining cheddar cheese and remaining butter on top. Cook for 30 minutes, tossing every 10 minutes. Serve.

Molasses Cashew Delight

Prep + Cook Time: 20 minutes | Serves: 4

Ingredients

3 cups cashews

3 tbsp liquid smoke

2 tsp salt

2 tbsp molasses

Directions

Preheat Cuisinart on Air Fry function to 360 F. In a bowl, add salt, liquid, molasses, and cashews; toss to coat thoroughly. Place the cashews in the frying baking tray and cook for 10 minutes, shaking every 5 minutes. Serve.

Ham and Cheese Grilled Sandwich

Prep + Cook Time: 15 minutes | Serves: 2

Ingredients

4 slices bread

¼ cup butter

2 slices ham

2 slices cheese

Directions

Preheat Cuisinart on Air Fry function to 360 F. Place 2 bread slices on a flat surface. Spread butter on the exposed surfaces. Lay cheese and ham on two of the slices. Cover with the other 2 slices to form sandwiches. Place the sandwiches in the cooking basket and cook for 5 minutes on Bake function. For additional crispiness, set on Toast function for 2 minutes.

Crispy Eggplant Fries

Prep + Cook Time: 20 minutes Serves: 2

Ingredients

1 eggplant, sliced

1 tsp olive oil

1 tsp soy sauce

Salt to taste

Directions

Preheat Cuisinart on Air Fry function to 400 F. Make a marinade of 1 tsp oil, soy sauce, and salt. Mix well. Add in the eggplant slices and let stand for 5 minutes. Place the prepared eggplant slices in the cooking basket and fit in the baking tray. Cook for 8 minutes. Serve warm.

Homemade Prosciutto Wrapped Cheese Sticks

Prep + Cook Time: 50 minutes | Serves: 6

Ingredients

1 lb cheddar cheese

12 slices of prosciutto

1 cup flour

2 eggs, beaten

4 tbsp olive oil

1 cup breadcrumbs

Directions

Cut the cheese into 6 equal sticks. Wrap each piece with 2 prosciutto slices. Place them in the freezer just enough to set. Preheat Cuisinart on Air Fry function to 390 F. Dip the croquettes into flour first, then in eggs, and coat with breadcrumbs. Drizzle the basket with oil and fit in the baking tray. Cook for 10 minutes or until golden. Serve.

Mom's Tarragon Chicken Breast Packets

Prep + Cook Time: 15 minutes | Serves: 2

Ingredients

2 chicken breasts

1 tbsp butter

Salt and black pepper to taste

¼ tsp dried tarragon

Preheat Cuisinart on Bake function to 380 F. Place each chicken breast on a 12x12 inches foil wrap. Top the chicken with tarragon and butter; season with salt and pepper. Wrap the foil around the chicken breast in a loose way to create a flow of air. Cook the in your Cuisinart oven for 15 minutes. Carefully unwrap and serve.

Poultry Recipes

Marinara Sauce Cheese Chicken

Prep + Cook Time: 25 minutes | Serves: 2

Ingredients

2 chicken breasts, sliced

1 egg, beaten

½ cup breadcrumbs

A pinch of salt and black pepper

2 tbsp tomato sauce

2 tbsp Romano cheese, grated

2 slices mozzarella cheese

Directions

Dip the breasts into the egg, then into the crumbs, and arrange in the basket. Fit in the baking tray and cook for 5 minutes at 400 F on Air Fry function. Turn and top with tomato sauce, Romano and mozzarella cheeses. Cook for 5 more minutes until the cheese is melted. Serve.

Honey & Garlic Chicken Thighs

Prep + Cook Time: 30 minutes | Serves: 4

Ingredients

4 thighs, skin-on

3 tbsp honey

2 tbsp Dijon mustard

½ tbsp garlic powder

Salt and black pepper to taste

Directions

In a bowl, mix honey, mustard, garlic, salt, and black pepper. Coat the thighs in the mixture and arrange them on the greased basket. Fit in the baking tray and cook for 16 minutes at 400 F on Air Fry function, turning once halfway through. Serve warm.

Parmesan Chicken Fingers with Plum Sauce

Prep + Cook Time: 20 minutes | Serves: 2

Ingredients

2 chicken breasts, cut in strips

3 tbsp Parmesan cheese, grated

¼ tbsp fresh chives, chopped

⅓ cup breadcrumbs

1 egg white

2 tbsp plum sauce, optional

½ tbsp fresh thyme, chopped

½ tbsp black pepper

1 tbsp water

Directions

Preheat Cuisinart on Air Fry function to 360 F. Mix the chives, Parmesan cheese, thyme, pepper and breadcrumbs. In another bowl, whisk the egg white and mix with the water. Dip the chicken strips into the egg mixture and then in the breadcrumb mixture. Place the strips in the greased basket and fit in the baking tray. Cook for 10 minutes, flipping once. Serve with plum sauce.

Herby Chicken with Lime

Prep + Cook Time: 30 minutes + chilling time| Serves: 4

1 (2 ½ lb) whole chicken

Salt and black pepper to taste

1 tbsp chili powder

1 tbsp garlic powder

4 tbsp oregano

2 tbsp cilantro powder

2 tbsp cumin powder

2 tbsp olive oil

4 tbsp paprika

1 lime, juiced

In a bowl, pour oregano, garlic powder, chili powder, ground cilantro, paprika, cumin, pepper, salt, and olive oil. Mix well and rub the mixture onto the chicken. Refrigerate for 20 minutes.

Preheat Cuisinart on Air Fry function to 350 F. Remove the chicken from the refrigerator; place in the greased basket and fit in the baking tray; cook for 20 minutes. Use a skewer to poke the chicken to ensure that it is clear of juices. If not, cook further for 5 to 10 minutes; let it rest for 10 minutes. Drizzle lime juice all over and serve with green salad.

Spicy Chicken Strips with Aioli Sauce

Prep + Cook Time: 15 minutes | Serves: 4

3 chicken breasts, cut into strips

2 tbsp olive oil

1 cup breadcrumbs

Salt and black pepper to taste

½ tbsp garlic powder

½ cup mayonnaise

1 tbsp lemon juice

½ tbsp ground chili

Mix breadcrumbs, salt, pepper, and garlic and spread onto a plate. Brush the chicken with olive oil then roll up in the breadcrumb mixture. Arrange on the oiled SirFryer basket and fit in the baking tray; cook for 10-12 minutes at 360 F on Air Fry function, turning once halfway through.

To prepare the aioli: mix well mayonnaise with lemon juice and ground chili. Serve the chicken with hot aioli.

Fried Chicken Tenderloins

Prep + Cook Time: 15 minutes | Serves: 4

Ingredients

8 chicken tenderloins

2 tbsp butter, softened

2 oz breadcrumbs

1 large egg, whisked

Directions

Preheat Cuisinart on Air Fry function to 380 F. Combine butter and breadcrumbs in a bowl. Keep mixing and stirring until the mixture gets crumbly. Dip the chicken in the egg, then in the crumb mix. Place in the greased basket and fit in the baking tray; cook for 10 minutes, flipping once until crispy. Set on Broil function for crispier taste. Serve.

Ham & Cheese Stuffed Chicken Breasts

Prep + Cook Time: 40 minutes | Serves: 4

Ingredients

4 skinless and boneless chicken breasts

4 slices ham

4 slices Swiss cheese

3 tbsp all-purpose flour

4 tbsp butter

1 tbsp paprika

1 tbsp chicken bouillon granules

½ cup dry white wine

1 cup heavy whipping cream

Directions

Preheat Cuisinart on Air Fry function to 380 F. Pound the chicken breasts and top with a slice of ham and Swiss cheese. Fold the edges of the chicken over the filling and secure the borders with toothpicks. In a medium bowl, combine the paprika and flour and coat in the chicken rolls. Fry the chicken in your Cuisinart for 20 minutes, turning once.

In a large skillet over low heat, melt the butter and add the heavy cream, bouillon granules, and wine; bring to a boil. Add in the chicken and let simmer for around 5-10 minutes. Serve.

Chicken Wrapped in Bacon

Prep + Cook Time: 20 minutes | Serves: 2

Ingredients

2 chicken breasts

8 oz onion and chive cream cheese

1 tbsp butter

6 turkey bacon

Salt to taste

1 tbsp fresh parsley, chopped

Juice from ½ lemon

Directions

Preheat on Air Fry function to 390 F. Stretch out the bacon slightly and lay them in 2 sets; 3 bacon strips together on each side. Place the chicken breast on each bacon set and use a knife to smear cream cheese on both. Share the butter on top and sprinkle with salt. Wrap the bacon around the chicken and secure the ends into the wrap.

Place the wrapped chicken in the AirFryer basket and fit in the baking tray; cook for 14 minutes. Turn the chicken halfway through. Remove the chicken to a serving platter and top with parsley and lemon juice. Serve with steamed greens.

Thyme Turkey Nuggets

Prep + Cook Time: 20 minutes | Serves: 2

Ingredients

8 oz turkey breast

1 egg, beaten

1 cup breadcrumbs

½ tsp dried thyme

Salt and black pepper to taste

Directions

Preheat Cuisinart on Air Fry function to 350 F. Pulse the turkey in a food processor and transfer to a bowl. Stir in thyme, salt, and pepper.

Form nugget-sized balls out of turkey mixture and dip in breadcrumbs, then in egg, and finally in the breadcrumbs again. Place the nuggets on a greased AirFryer basket and fit in the baking tray. Cook for 10 minutes, shaking once until golden brown. Serve warm.

Cayenne Chicken Drumsticks

Prep + Cook Time: 50 minutes | Serves: 4

Ingredients

8 chicken drumsticks

2 tbsp oregano

2 tbsp thyme

2 oz oats

¼ cup milk

¼ steamed cauliflower florets

1 egg

1 tbsp ground cayenne pepper

Salt and black pepper to taste

Directions

Preheat Cuisinart on Air Fry function to 350 F. Season the drumsticks with salt and pepper; rub them with the milk. Place all the other ingredients except the egg in a food processor. Process until smooth. Dip drumsticks in the egg first and then in the oat mixture. Arrange on the greased AitirFryer basket and fit in the baking tray. Cook for 20 minutes until golden brown.

Fruity Chicken Breasts with BBQ Sauce

Prep + Cook Time: 20 minutes | Serves: 2

Ingredients

2 chicken breasts, cubed

2 green bell peppers, sliced

½ onion, sliced

1 can drain pineapple chunks

½ cup barbecue sauce

Directions

Preheat Cuisinart on Bake function to 370 F. Thread the green bell peppers, chicken cubes, onions, and pineapple chunks on the skewers. Brush with barbecue sauce and cook in your Cuisinart for 20 minutes until slightly crispy. Serve.

Herby Stuffed Turkey Breast

Prep + Cook Time: 35 minutes | Serves: 4

Ingredients

1 pound turkey breast

1 ham slice

1 slice cheddar cheese

2 oz breadcrumbs

1 tbsp cream cheese

½ tsp garlic powder

1 tbsp fresh thyme, chopped

1 tbsp fresh tarragon, chopped

1 egg, beaten

Salt and black pepper to taste

Directions

Preheat Cuisinart on Air Fry function to 350 F. Cut the turkey in the middle; that way so you can add ingredients in the center. Season with salt, pepper, thyme, and tarragon. Combine cream cheese and garlic powder in a bowl.

Spread the mixture on the inside of the breast. Place half cheddar slice and half ham slice in the center of each breast. Dip in the egg first, then sprinkle with breadcrumbs. Cook on the baking tray for 30 minutes, flipping once.

Mango Marinated Chicken Breasts

Prep + Cook Time: 20 minutes + marinating time| Serves: 2

Ingredients

2 chicken breasts, cubed

1 large mango, cubed

1 red pepper, chopped

2 tbsp balsamic vinegar

5 tbsp olive oil

2 garlic cloves, minced

1 tbsp fresh parsley, chopped

Salt to taste

Directions

In a bowl, mix mango, garlic, red pepper, olive oil, salt, and balsamic vinegar. Add the mixture to a blender and pulse until smooth. Transfer to a bowl and add in the chicken cubes. Toss to coat and place in the fridge for 30 minutes.

Preheat Cuisinart on Air Fry function to 360 F. Remove the chicken from the fridge and place cubes in the greased basket. Fit in the baking tray and cook in the air fryer oven for 12 minutes, shaking once. Garnish with parsley and serve.

Sticky Chinese-Style Chicken

Prep + Cook Time: 25 minutes | Serves: 3

Ingredients

1 lb chicken wingettes

1 tbsp cilantro leaves, chopped

Salt and black pepper, to taste

1 tbsp roasted peanuts, chopped

½ tbsp apple cider vinegar

1 garlic clove, minced

½ tbsp chili sauce

1 ginger, minced

1 ½ tbsp soy sauce

2 ½ tbsp honey

Directions

In a bowl, mix ginger, garlic, chili sauce, honey, soy sauce, cilantro, salt, pepper, and vinegar. Add in the chicken toss to coat. Place the prepared chicken onto the greased basket and fit in the baking tray; cook for 20 minutes at 360 F on Air Fry function. Serve sprinkled with peanuts.

Worcestershire Chicken Breasts

Prep + Cook Time: 20 minutes | Serves: 4

Ingredients

¼ cup flour

½ tbsp flour

4 chicken breasts, sliced

1 tbsp Worcestershire sauce

3 tbsp olive oil

¼ cup onions, chopped

1 ½ cups brown sugar

¼ cup yellow mustard

¾ cup water

½ cup ketchup

Directions

In a bowl, mix flour, salt, and pepper. Cover the chicken slices with flour mixture and drizzle with olive oil. In another bowl, mix brown sugar, water, ketchup, onion, mustard, Worcestershire sauce, and salt. Add in the chicken and let sit for 10 minutes.

Preheat Cuisinart on Air Fry function to 360 F. Remove the chicken slices from the marinade and place them in the greased basket. Fit in baking tray and cook for 15 minutes. Serve.

Korean-Style Chicken Wings

Prep + Cook Time: 20 minutes | Serves: 4

1 pound chicken wings

8 oz flour

8 oz breadcrumbs

3 beaten eggs

4 tbsp canola oil

Salt and black pepper to taste

2 tbsp sesame seeds

2 tbsp Korean red pepper paste

1 tbsp apple cider vinegar

2 tbsp honey

1 tbsp soy sauce

Sesame seeds, to serve

Separate the chicken wings into winglets and drumettes. In a bowl, mix salt, olive oil, and pepper. Coat the chicken with flour followed by eggs and breadcrumbs. Place in the basket and fit in the baking tray. Oil with cooking spray and cook for 15 minutes on Air Fry mode at 350 F.

Mix red pepper paste, apple cider vinegar, soy sauce, honey, and ¼ cup of water in a saucepan and bring to a boil over medium heat. Simmer until the sauce thickens, about 3-4 minutes. Pour the sauce over the chicken pieces. Garnish with sesame seeds and serve.

Savory Honey & Garlic Chicken

Prep + Cook Time: 20 minutes + marinating time| Serves: 2

2 chicken drumsticks, skin removed

2 tbsp olive oil

2 tbsp honey

½ tbsp garlic, minced

Add garlic, olive oil, and honey to a sealable zip bag. Add chicken and toss to coat; set aside for 30 minutes. Add the coated chicken to the basket and fit in the baking sheet; cook for 15 minutes at 400 F on Air Fry function, flipping once. Serve and enjoy!

Shrimp Paste Chicken

Prep + Cook Time: 30 minutes | Serves: 2

6 chicken wings

½ tbsp sugar

2 tbsp cornflour

1 tbsp white wine

1 tbsp shrimp paste

1 tbsp grated ginger

½ tbsp olive oil

In a bowl, mix shrimp paste, olive oil, ginger, white wine, and sugar. Cover the chicken wings with the prepared marinade and roll in the flour.

Place the chicken in the greased baking dish and cook in your Cuisinart for 20 minutes at 350 F on Air Fry function. Serve.

Sherry Grilled Chicken

Prep + Cook Time: 25 minutes | Serves: 2

Ingredients

2 chicken breasts, cubed

2 garlic clove, minced

½ cup ketchup

½ tbsp ginger, minced

½ cup soy sauce

2 tbsp sherry

½ cup pineapple juice

2 tbsp apple cider vinegar

½ cup brown sugar

Directions

In a bowl, mix ketchup, pineapple juice, sugar, cider vinegar, and ginger. Heat the mixture in a frying pan over low heat. Cover chicken with the soy sauce and sherry; pour the hot sauce on top. Set aside for 15 minutes to marinate.

Preheat your Cuisinart oven on Broil function to 360 F. Remove the chicken from the marinade, pat dry, and place it in the greased basket. Fit in a baking tray and cook for 15 minutes.

Hot Chicken Wings

Prep + Cook Time: 20 minutes + chilling time| Serves: 2

Ingredients

8 chicken wings

1 tbsp water

2 tbsp potato starch

2 tbsp hot curry paste

½ tbsp baking powder

Directions

Combine hot curry paste and water in a small bowl. Add in the wings toss to coat. Cover the bowl with plastic wrap and refrigerate for 30 minutes.

Preheat Cuisinart on Air Fry function to 370 degrees. In a bowl, mix the baking powder with potato starch. Remove the wings from the fridge and dip them in the starch mixture.

Place on a lined baking dish and cook in your Cuisinart for 7 minutes. Flip over and cook for 5 minutes.

Pineapple & Ginger Chicken Kabobs

Prep + Cook Time: 20 minutes | Serves: 2

Ingredients

2 chicken breasts, cut into 2-inch pieces

½ cup soy sauce

½ cup pineapple juice

¼ cup sesame oil

4 cloves garlic, chopped

1 tbsp fresh ginger, grated

4 scallions, chopped

2 tbsp toasted sesame seeds

A pinch of black pepper

Directions

In a bowl, toss to coat all the ingredients except the chicken. Let sit for 10 minutes.

Preheat your Cuisinart oven on Air Fry function to 390 F. Remove the chicken pieces and pat them dry using paper towels. Thread the chicken pieces onto skewers and trim any fat. Place in the AirFryer basket and fit in the baking tray. Cook for 7-10 minutes, flipping once. Serve.

Mustardy Chicken

Prep + Cook Time: 20 minutes | Serves: 4

Ingredients

1 tsp garlic powder

4 chicken breasts, sliced

1 tbsp fresh thyme, chopped

½ cup dry white wine

Salt and black pepper to taste

½ cup Dijon mustard

2 cups breadcrumbs

1 tbsp lemon zest

2 tbsp olive oil

Directions

In a bowl, mix garlic, breadcrumbs, olive oil, lemon zest, salt, and pepper. In another bowl, mix mustard and wine.

Dip the chicken slices in the wine mixture and then coat in the crumb mixture. Place the prepared chicken in the greased basket and fit in the baking tray; cook for 15 minutes at 350 F on Air Fry function, shaking once until golden brown. Serve.

Sweet Chicken Drumsticks

Prep + Cook Time: 20 minutes + marinating time| Serves: 2

Ingredients

2 chicken drumsticks, skin removed

2 tbsp olive oil

2 tbsp honey

½ tbsp garlic, minced

Directions

Add all the ingredients to a resealable bag; massage until well-coated. Allow the chicken to marinate for 30 minutes in the fridge.

Preheat Cuisinart on Air Fry function to 390 F. Remove the chicken drumsticks from the fridge and add them to the greased basket. Fit in the baking tray and cook for 15 minutes, shaking once. Serve hot.

Chicken with Peppercorns & Lemon

Prep + Cook Time: 20 minutes | Serves: 1

Ingredients

1 chicken breast

2 lemon, juiced and rind reserved

1 tbsp chicken seasoning

1 tbsp garlic puree

A handful of peppercorns

Salt and black pepper to taste

Directions

Place a silver foil sheet on a flat surface. Add all seasonings alongside the lemon rind. Lay the chicken breast onto a chopping board and trim any fat.

Season with salt and pepper. Rub the chicken with the seasoning on both sides. Place on the silver foil sheet. Seal tightly and flatten with a rolling pin.

Place the breast in the basket and fit in the baking tray; cook for 15 minutes at 350 F on Air Fry function. Serve hot.

Cheesy Chicken Escallops

Prep + Cook Time: 10 minutes | Serves: 4

Ingredients

4 skinless chicken breasts

2 ½ oz panko breadcrumbs

1 ounce Parmesan cheese, grated

6 sage leaves, chopped

1 ¼ ounces flour

2 beaten eggs

Directions

Place the chicken breasts between a cling film, beat well using a rolling pin until a ½ inch thickness is achieved.

In a bowl, add Parmesan cheese, sage, and breadcrumbs. Dredge the chicken into the seasoned flour and then into the eggs. Finally, coat in the breadcrumbs.

Spray the chicken breasts with cooking spray and cook in your Cuisinart oven for 14-16 minutes at 350 F on Air Fry function.

Savory Buffalo Chicken

Prep + Cook Time: 35 minutes | Serves: 4

Ingredients

2 pounds chicken wings

½ cup cayenne pepper sauce

½ cup coconut oil

1 tbsp Worcestershire sauce

1 tbsp kosher salt

In a bowl, mix cayenne pepper sauce, coconut oil, Worcestershire sauce, and salt; set aside. Place chicken in the Air Fryer basket and fit in the baking tray. Cook for 25 minutes at 380 F on Air Fy function. Transfer to a large-sized plate and drizzle with the prepared sauce to serve.

Garlic-Buttery Chicken Wings

Prep + Cook Time: 20 minutes | Serves: 4

12 chicken wings

¼ cup butter

¼ cup honey

½ tbsp salt

4 garlic cloves, minced

¾ cup potato starch

Preheat Cuisinart on Air Fry function to 370 F. Coat chicken with potato starch. Transfer to the greased Air Fryer basket and fit in the baking tray. Cook for 5 minutes. Whisk the rest of the ingredients in a bowl. Pour the sauce over the wings and serve.

Rosemary Chicken Breasts

Prep + Cook Time: 15minutes | Serves: 2

2 chicken breasts

Salt and black pepper to taste

½ cup dried rosemary

1 tbsp butter, melted

Preheat Cuisinart on Air Fry function to 390 F. Lay a foil on a flat surface. Place the breasts on the foil, sprinkle with rosemary, tarragon, salt, and pepper and and drizzle the butter.

Wrap the foil around the breasts. Place the wrapped chicken in the AirFryer basket and fit in the baking tray; cook for 12 minutes. Remove and carefully unwrap. Serve with the sauce extract and steamed veggies.

Enchilada Cheese Chicken

Prep + Cook Time: 25 minutes | Serves: 3

3 cups chicken breasts, chopped

2 cups cheese, grated

½ cup salsa

1 can green chilies, chopped

12 flour tortillas

2 cans enchilada sauce

In a bowl, mix salsa and enchilada sauce. Toss in the chopped chicken to coat. Place the chicken on the tortillas and roll; top with cheese. Place the prepared tortillas in a baking tray and cook for 15-18 minutes at 400 F on Bake function. Serve with guacamole and hot dips!

Basil Mozzarella Chicken

Prep + Cook Time: 25 minutes | Serves: 4

Ingredients

4 chicken breasts, cubed

4 basil leaves

¼ cup balsamic vinegar

4 slices tomato

1 tbsp butter

4 slices mozzarella cheese

Directions

Heat butter and balsamic vinegar in a pan over medium heat. Pour over the chicken. Place the chicken in a baking pan and cook for 20 minutes at 400 F on Bake function. Top with cheese, and Bake for 1 minute until the cheese melts. Cover with basil and tomato slices and serve.

Lime-Chili Chicken Wings

Prep + Cook Time: 25 minutes | Serves: 2

Ingredients

9 chicken wings

2 tbsp hot chili sauce

½ tbsp lime juice

½ tbsp honey

½ tbsp kosher salt

½ tbsp black pepper

Directions

Preheat Cuisinart on Air Fry function to 350 F. Mix the lime juice, honey, and chili sauce. Toss the mixture over the chicken wings. Put the chicken wings in the basket and fit in the baking tray; cook for 25 minutes. Shake every 5 minutes. Serve.

Chicken with Avocado & Radish Bowl

Prep + Cook Time: 20 minutes | Serves: 2

Ingredients

2 chicken breasts

1 avocado, sliced

4 radishes, sliced

1 tbsp chopped parsley

Salt and black pepper to taste

Directions

Preheat Cuisinart on Air Fry function to 300 F. Cut the chicken into small cubes. Combine all ingredients in a bowl and transfer to the Air Fryer pan. Cook for 14 minutes, shaking once. Serve with cooked rice or fried red kidney beans.

Delicious Coconut Chicken Casserole

Prep + Cook Time: 20 minutes | Serves: 4

Ingredients

2 large eggs, beaten

2 tbsp garlic powder

Salt and black pepper to taste

¾ cup breadcrumbs

¾ cup shredded coconut

1 pound chicken tenders

Directions

Preheat your Cuisinart on Air Fry function to 400 F. Spray a baking sheet with cooking spray. In a deep dish, whisk garlic powder, eggs, pepper, and salt. In another bowl, mix the breadcrumbs and coconut. Dip your chicken tenders in egg mixture, then in the coconut mix; shake off any excess. Place the prepared chicken tenders in the greased basket and fit in the baking tray; cook for 12-14 minutes until golden brown. Serve.

Savory Chicken with Onion

Prep + Cook Time: 20 minutes | Serves: 4

Ingredients

4 chicken breasts, cubed

1 ½ cup onion soup mix

1 cup mushroom soup

½ cup heavy cream

Directions

Preheat your Cuisinart oven to 400 F on Bake function. Add mushrooms, onion mix, and heavy cream in a frying pan. Heat on low heat for 1 minute. Pour the warm mixture over chicken and allow to sit for 25 minutes. Place the marinated chicken in the basket and fit in the baking tray; cook for 15 minutes. Serve and enjoy!

Basil Cheese Chicken

Prep + Cook Time: 20 minutes | Serves: 4

Ingredients

4 chicken breasts, cubed

1 tbsp garlic powder

1 cup mayonnaise

½ tsp pepper

½ cup soft cheese

½ tbsp salt

Chopped basil for garnish

Directions

In a bowl, mix cheese, mayonnaise, garlic powder, and salt to form a marinade. Cover your chicken with the marinade. Place the marinated chicken in the basket and fit in the baking tray; cook for 15 minutes at 380 F on Air Fry function. Serve garnished with chopped fresh basil.

Cayenne Chicken with Coconut Flakes

Prep + Cook Time: 25 minutes | Serves: 4

3 chicken breasts, cubed

3 cups coconut flakes

3 whole eggs, beaten

½ cup cornstarch

Salt and black pepper to taste

1 tbsp cayenne pepper

In a bowl, mix salt, cornstarch, cayenne and black peppers. In another bowl, mix beaten eggs with coconut flakes. Dip the chicken in pepper mix, then in the egg mix. Cover with foil and place in the basket. Fit in the baking tray and cook for 20 minutes at 350 F on Air Fry function.

Honey Chicken Wings

Prep + Cook Time: 25 minutes | Serves: 4

8 chicken drumsticks

2 tbsp sesame oil

4 tbsp honey

3 tbsp light soy sauce

2 crushed garlic clove

1 small knob fresh ginger, grated

1 small bunch cilantro, chopped

2 tbsp sesame seeds, toasted

Add all ingredients in a bowl, except sesame and cilantro. Massage until drumsticks are well coated. Preheat Cuisinart to 400 F on Air Fry. Place the drumsticks in the basket and fit in the baking tray; cook for 15 minutes, flipping once. Sprinkle with sesame seeds and cilantro. Serve.

Ginger Chicken Wings

Prep + Cook Time: 25 minutes | Serves: 3

1 pound chicken wings

1 tbsp cilantro

Salt and black pepper to taste

1 garlic clove, minced

1 tbsp yogurt

2 tbsp honey

½ tbsp vinegar

½ tbsp ginger, minced

Preheat Cuisinart on Air Fry to 360 F. Season wings with salt and pepper, place them in the basket and fit in the baking tray. Cook for 15 minutes, shaking once. In a bowl, mix the remaining ingredients. Top the chicken with sauce and cook for 5 more minutes. Serve.

Parmesan Chicken Cutlets

Prep + Cook Time: 30 minutes | Serves: 4

Ingredients

¼ cup Parmesan cheese, grated

4 chicken cutlets

⅛ tbsp paprika

2 tbsp panko breadcrumbs

½ tbsp garlic powder

2 large eggs, beaten

Directions

In a bowl, mix Parmesan cheese, breadcrumbs, garlic powder, and paprika. Add eggs to another bowl. Dip the chicken in eggs, dredge them in cheese mixture and place them in the basket and fit in the baking tray. Cook for 20-25 minutes on Air Fry function at 400 F.

Buttered Crispy Turkey

Prep + Cook Time: 25 minutes | Serves: 4

Ingredients

1 pound turkey breast, halved

2 cups panko breadcrumbs

Salt and black pepper to taste

½ tsp cayenne pepper

1 stick butter, melted

Directions

In a bowl, combine the breadcrumbs, salt, cayenne and black peppers. Brush the butter onto the turkey breast and coat in the crumb mixture. Transfer to a lined baking dish. Cook in your Cuisinart for 15 minutes at 390 F. Serve warm.

Meat Recipes

Homemade Pork Ratatouille

Prep + Cook Time: 25 minutes | Serves: 4

Ingredients

4 pork sausages

For Ratatouille

1 red pepper, chopped

2 zucchinis, chopped

1 eggplant, chopped

1 medium red onion, chopped

1 tbsp olive oil

1-ounce butterbean, drained

15 oz tomatoes, chopped

1 tbsp balsamic vinegar

2 garlic cloves, minced

1 red chili, chopped

Directions

Mix red pepper, eggplant, olive oil, onion, and zucchinis and add to a baking pan. Roast for 20 minutes on Bake function at 390 F. Lower temperature to 350 F.

Place a saucepan over medium heat and add in the vegetables and the remaining ratatouille ingredients. Mix well and bring to a boil. Let the mixture simmer for 10 minutes; season.

Add sausages to the frying basket and fit in the baking tray; cook for 10 minutes on Air Fry function at 350 F. Serve the sausages with ratatouille.

Sweet Marinaded Pork Chops

Prep + Cook Time: 15 minutes | Serves: 3

Ingredients

3 pork chops, ½-inch thick

Salt and black pepper to taste to season

1 tbsp maple syrup

1 ½ tbsp minced garlic

3 tbsp mustard

Directions

In a bowl, add maple syrup, garlic, mustard, salt, and pepper; mix well. Add in the pork and toss to coat. Slide-out the basket and place the chops inside. Fit in the baking tray and cook in your Cuisinart at 350 F for 6 minutes on Air Fry function.

Flip the chops with a spatula and cook further for 6 minutes. Once ready, remove them to a platter and serve with steamed asparagus.

Beef Rolls with Pesto & Spinach

Prep + Cook Time: 30 minutes | Serves: 4

Ingredients

2 pounds beef steaks, sliced

Salt and black pepper to taste

3 tbsp pesto

6 slices mozzarella cheese

¾ cup spinach, chopped

3 oz bell pepper, deseeded and sliced

Top the meat with pesto, mozzarella cheese, spinach, and bell pepper. Roll up the slices and secure using a toothpick. Season with salt and pepper. Place the slices in the basket and fit in the baking tray; cook for 15 minutes on Air Fry function at 400 F, turning once. Serve immediately!

Savory Pulled Pork with Cheddar & Bacon

Prep + Cook Time: 50 minutes | Serves: 2

Ingredients

1 pork steak

1 tsp steak seasoning

Salt and black pepper to taste

5 thick bacon slices, chopped

1 cup grated Cheddar cheese

½ tbsp Worcestershire sauce

2 bread buns, halved

Directions

Preheat Cuisinart on Bake function to 380 F. Place the pork steak in the baking pan and season with pepper, salt, and steak seasoning. Cook for 20-22 minutes, turning once. Remove the steak onto a chopping board and using two forks, shred it into pieces. Return to the baking pan.

Place the bacon in a skillet over medium heat and cook for 5 minutes until crispy. Add the bacon to the pork pan and stir. Mix in Worcestershire sauce, cheddar cheese, salt, and pepper.

Place again the pan in the oven and cook for 4 minutes. Slide-out, stir with a spoon, and cook further for 1 minute. Spoon the meat into the halved buns and serve with tomato dip.

Italian-Style Pork Chops

Prep + Cook Time: 30 minutes + marinating time | Serves: 4

Ingredients

4 pork chops, sliced

2 tbsp olive oil

Salt and black pepper to taste

1 whole egg, beaten

1 tbsp flour

1 cup breadcrumbs

1 tsp Italian herbs

Directions

In a bowl, place olive oil, salt, and pepper and mix well. Stir in the pork, cover, and let it marinate for 15 minutes. Place the beaten egg in a plate. In a separate plate, add the breadcrumbs

Preheat Cuisinart on Air Fry function to 400 F. Dip the pork in the egg and then into the breadcrumbs. Place in the cooking basket and fit in the baking tray; cook for 20 minutes, shaking once. Serve warm.

Tamarind Pork Chops with Green Beans

Prep + Cook Time: 30 minutes + marinating time| Serves: 4

2 tbsp tamarind paste

½ lb green beans, trimmed

1 tbsp garlic, minced

½ cup green mole sauce

3 tbsp corn syrup

1 tbsp olive oil

2 tbsp molasses

4 tbsp southwest seasoning

2 tbsp ketchup

4 pork chops

In a bowl, mix all the ingredients, except for potatoes, pork chops, and mole sauce. Add in 2 tbsp of water. Let the pork chops marinate in the mixture for 30 minutes.

Place pork chops in the basket and fit in the baking tray; cook for 25 minutes on Air Fry function at 350 F. Blanch the green beans in salted water in a pot over medium heat for 2-3 minutes until tender. Drain and season with salt and pepper. Serve the pork with green beans and mole sauce.

Almond & Apple Pork Balls

Prep + Cook Time: 40 minutes | Serves: 4

16 oz sausage meat

1 whole egg, beaten

4 oz onion, chopped

2 tbsp almonds, chopped

Salt and black pepper to taste

4 oz apples, sliced

Preheat Cuisinart oven to 350 F on Air Fry function. In a bowl, mix onion, almonds, apples, egg, pepper, and salt. Add the almond mixture and sausages in a Ziploc bag. Mix to coat well and set aside for 15 minutes.

Form balls from the mixture and add them to greased frying basket. Fit in the baking tray and cook for 25 minutes, shaking once. Serve warm.

Teriyaki Pork Ribs with Tomato Sauce

Prep + Cook Time: 20 minutes + marinating time| Serves: 3

1 pound pork ribs

Salt and black pepper to taste

1 tbsp sugar

1 tsp ginger juice

1 tsp five-spice powder

1 tbsp teriyaki sauce

1 tbsp soy sauce

1 garlic clove, minced

2 tbsp honey

1 tbsp tomato sauce

1 tbsp olive oil

In a bowl, mix pepper, sugar, five-spice powder, salt, ginger juice, and teriyaki sauce. Add pork ribs to the marinade and let sit for 2 hours.

Add ribs to the greased basket and fit in the baking tray; cook for 8 minutes on Air Fry function at 350 F. In a separate bowl, mix soy sauce, garlic, honey, 1 tbsp of water, and tomato sauce.

In a pan over medium heat, heat olive oil and fry garlic for 30 seconds. Add fried pork ribs and pour in the sauce. Stir-fry for a few minutes and serve.

Corned Beef with Carrots

Prep + Cook Time: 35 minutes + marinating time| Serves: 4

Ingredients

1 tbsp beef spice

1 onion, chopped

2 carrots, chopped

12 oz bottle beer

1 ½ cups chicken broth

2 pounds corned beef

Directions

Cover beef with beer and let sit for 20 minutes. Place carrots, onion, and beef in a pot and heat over high heat. Add in broth and bring to a boil. Drain and set aside. Season with beef spice. Place the meat and veggies in the cooking basket and fit in the baking tray; cook for 30 minutes at 400 F on Air Fry function. Serve.

Chili Pork Chops with Tomatoes & Rice

Prep + Cook Time: 40 minutes + marinating time| Serves: 4

Ingredients

4 pork chops

1 lime juice

Salt and black pepper to taste

1 tsp garlic powder

1 ½ cups white rice, cooked

2 tbsp olive oil

1 can (14.5 oz) tomato sauce

1 onion, chopped

3 garlic cloves, minced

½ tsp oregano

1 tsp chipotle chili

Directions

Season pork with salt, pepper, and garlic powder. In a bowl, mix onion, garlic, chipotle, oregano, and tomato sauce. Add in the pork. Let sit for 1 hour. Then remove from the mixture and place in the basket. Fit in the baking tray and cook for 25 minutes on Air Fry at 350 F. Serve with rice.

Cocktail Franks in Blanket

Prep + Cook Time: 20 minutes | Serves: 4

Ingredients

12 oz cocktail franks

8 oz can crescent rolls

Directions

Use a paper towel to pat the cocktail franks to drain completely. Cut the dough in 1 by 1.5-inch rectangles using a knife. Gently roll the franks in the strips, making sure the ends are visible Place in freezer for 5 minutes.

Preheat Cuisinart oven to 330 F on Air Fry function. Take the franks out of the freezer and place them in the frying basket to cook for 8-10 minutes. Increase temperature to 390 F and cook for another 3 minutes until a fine golden texture appears. Serve.

Smoked Ham with Pears

Prep + Cook Time: 30 minutes | Serves: 4

Ingredients

15 oz pears, halved

2 lb smoked ham, or similar size that fits

1 ½ cups brown sugar

¾ tbsp allspice

1 tbsp apple cider vinegar

1 tsp black pepper

1 tsp vanilla extract

Directions

Preheat your Cuisinart to 330 F on Air Fry function. Place the ham in a baking dish. In a bowl, mix pears, brown sugar, cider vinegar, vanilla extract, pepper, and allspice.

Place the mixture in a frying pan and fry for 2-3 minutes. Pour the mixture over ham. Insert the baking dish in your Cuisinart and cook for 15 minutes. Serve the ham with hot sauce!

Morning Ham & Cheese Sandwich

Prep + Cook Time: 15 minutes | Serves: 4

Ingredients

8 slices whole wheat bread

4 slices lean pork ham

4 slices cheese

8 slices tomato

Directions

Lay four slices of bread on a flat surface. Spread the slices with cheese, tomato, turkey, and ham. Cover with the remaining slices to form sandwiches. Add the sandwiches to the cooking basket and cook for 10 minutes at 360 F on Air Fry function. Serve.

Sage Sausage Balls

Prep + Cook Time: 20 minutes | Serves: 4

Ingredients

6 oz pork sausages, sliced

Salt and black pepper to taste

1 cup onions, chopped

3 tbsp breadcrumbs

½ tsp garlic puree

1 tsp sage

Directions

In a bowl, mix onions, sausages, sage, garlic puree, salt, and pepper. Form balls out of the mixture and roll in breadcrumbs. Add the balls to the cooking basket and fit in the baking tray; cook for 15 minutes on Air Fry function at 340 F, shaking once. Serve and enjoy!

Cheese Breaded Pork

Prep + Cook Time: 15 minutes | Serves: 4

Ingredients

4 pork chops

6 tbsp seasoned breadcrumbs

2 tbsp Parmesan cheese, grated

1 tbsp melted butter

½ cup mozzarella cheese, shredded

1 tbsp marinara sauce

Directions

Grease the cooking basket with cooking spray. In a small bowl, mix breadcrumbs and Parmesan cheese. Brush the pork with butter and dredge into the breadcrumbs.

Add pork to the basket and fit in the baking tray; cook for 8 minutes at 400 F on Air Fry function. Turn and top with marinara sauce and mozzarella cheese; cook for 5 more minutes. Serve.

Pork Belly with Honey

Prep + Cook Time: 35 minutes | Serves: 4

Ingredients

2 pounds pork belly

Salt and black pepper to taste

1 tbsp olive oil

3 tbsp honey

Directions

Season the pork belly with salt and pepper. Grease a baking pan with oil. Add seasoned meat and cook for 15 minutes at 400 F on Air Fry function. Brush with honey and cook for 10 minutes.

Grandma's Ground Beef Balls

Prep + Cook Time: 15 minutes | Serves: 4

Ingredients

1 pound ground beef

1 tbsp olive oil

1 large red onion, chopped

1 tsp garlic, minced

2 whole eggs, beaten

Salt and black pepper to taste

Directions

Place a skillet over medium heat and warm the oil. Add in onion and garlic and sauté for 3 minutes until tender. Remove to a bowl to cool. Add in the ground beef and egg and mix well.

Season with salt and pepper. Roll the mixture into golf-sized balls and place them in the greased frying basket. Fit in the baking tray and cook for 15 minutes on Air Fry function at 350 F. Serve.

Swiss Cheese Ham Muffins

Prep + Cook Time: 25 minutes | Serves: 8

Ingredients

4 whole eggs, beaten

3 oz ham

1 cup milk

1 ½ cups Swiss cheese, grated

Salt and black pepper to taste

¼ cup green onion, chopped

Directions

Preheat your Cuisinart to 350 F on Air Fry. In a bowl, mix eggs, onion, salt, cheese, pepper, and milk. Prepare baking forms and place ham slices in each one. Top with the egg mixture.

Place the muffin forms in the baking tray and cook for 15 minutes. Let cool for 10 minutes. Serve.

Amazing Bacon & Potato Platter

Prep + Cook Time: 40 minutes | Serves: 4

Ingredients

4 potatoes, halved

6 garlic cloves, squashed

4 streaky cut rashers bacon

1 tbsp olive oil

Directions

In a mixing bowl, mix garlic, bacon, potatoes, and olive oil; toss to coat. Place the mixture in the basket and fit in the baking tray; roast for 25-30 minutes at 400 F on Air Fry, shaking once.

Party Stuffed Pork Chops

Prep + Cook Time: 30 minutes + marinating time| Serves: 4

Ingredients

4 pork chops

Salt and black pepper to taste

4 cups stuffing mix

2 tbsp olive oil

4 garlic cloves, minced

2 tbsp sage leaves

Directions

Cut a hole in pork chops and fill chops with stuffing mix. In a bowl, mix sage leaves, garlic cloves, olive oil, salt, and pepper. Cover chops with marinade and let sit for 30 minutes. Place the chops in the cooking basket and fit in the baking tray; cook for 25 minutes on Air Fry function at 350 F, flipping once. Serve and enjoy!

Cheddar Pork Meatballs

Prep + Cook Time: 25 minutes | Serves: 4

Ingredients

1 lb ground pork

1 large onion, chopped

½ tsp maple syrup

2 tsp mustard

Salt and black pepper to taste

2 tbsp grated Cheddar cheese

Directions

In a bowl, add ground pork, onion, maple syrup, mustard, salt, pepper, and cheddar cheese and mix well. Use your hands to form small balls.

Place in the Cuisinart Air Fryer basket and fit in the baking tray; cook at 400 F for 10 minutes on Air Fry function. Slide out the basket and shake; cook further for 5 minutes. Remove them onto a wire rack and serve with zoodles and marinara sauce.

Fish & Seafood Recipes

Cheesy Tilapia Fillets

Prep + Cook Time: 15 minutes | Serves: 4

Ingredients

¾ cup grated Parmesan cheese

1 tbsp olive oil

2 tsp paprika

1 tbsp chopped parsley

¼ tsp garlic powder

4 tilapia fillets

Directions

Preheat Cuisinart on Air Fry function to 350 F. Mix parsley, Parmesan cheese, garlic, and paprika in a bowl. Brush the olive oil over the fillets and then coat with the Parmesan mixture. Place the tilapia onto a lined baking sheet and cook for 8-10 minutes, turning once. Serve.

Simple Lemon Salmon

Prep + Cook Time: 20 minutes | Serves: 2

Ingredients

2 salmon fillets

Salt to taste

Zest of a lemon

Directions

Spray the fillets with olive oil and rub them with salt and lemon zest. Line baking paper in a baking dish. Cook the fillets in your Cuisinart for 10 minutes at 360 F on Air Fry, turning once.

Chili-Rubbed Jumbo Shrimp

Prep + Cook Time: 10 minutes | Serves: 2 to 3

Ingredients

1 lb jumbo shrimp

Salt to taste

¼ tsp old bay seasoning

⅓ tsp smoked paprika

¼ tsp chili powder

1 tbsp olive oil

Directions

Preheat Cuisinart on Air Fry function to 390 F. In a bowl, add the shrimp, paprika, olive oil, salt, old bay seasoning, and chili powder; mix well. Place the shrimp in the basket and fit in the baking tray. Cook for 5 minutes, flipping once. Serve with mayo and rice.

Rosemary Buttered Prawns

Prep + Cook Time: 15 minutes + marinating time| Serves: 2

Ingredients

8 large prawns

1 rosemary sprig, chopped

½ tbsp melted butter

Salt and black pepper to taste

Directions

Combine butter, rosemary, salt, and pepper in a bowl. Add in the prawns and mix to coat. Cover the bowl and refrigerate for 1 hour.

Preheat Cuisinart on Air Fry function to 350 F Remove the prawns from the fridge and place them in the basket. Fit in the baking tray and cook for 10 minutes, flipping once. Serve.

Parmesan Fish with Pine Nuts

Prep + Cook Time: 15 minutes | Serves: 4

Ingredients

2 tbsp fresh basil, chopped

2 garlic cloves, minced

2 tbsp olive oil

1 tbsp Parmesan cheese, grated

salt and black pepper to taste

2 tbsp pine nuts

4 white fish fillets

2 tbsp olive oil

Directions

Preheat Cuisinart on Air Fry function to 350 F. Season the fish with salt and pepper. Place in the greased basket and fit in the baking tray. Cook the fillets for 8 minutes, flipping once. In a bowl, add basil, olive oil, pine nuts, garlic, and Parmesan cheese; mix well. Serve with the fish.

Delightful Catfish Fillets

Prep + Cook Time: 25 minutes | Serves: 4

Ingredients

4 catfish fillets

¼ cup seasoned fish fry

1 tbsp olive oil

1 tbsp parsley, chopped

Directions

Add seasoned fish fry and catfish fillets in a large Ziploc bag and massage well to coat. Place the fillets in your Cuisinart Air Fryer basket and fit in the baking tray; cook for 10 minutes at 360 F on Air Fry function. Flip the fish and cook for 2-3 more minutes. Top with parsley and serve.

Shrimp with Smoked Paprika & Cayenne Pepper

Prep + Cook Time: 10 minutes | Serves: 3

Ingredients

6 oz tiger shrimp, 12 to 16 pieces

1 tbsp olive oil

½ a tbsp old bay seasoning

¼ a tbsp cayenne pepper

¼ a tbsp smoked paprika

A pinch of sea salt

Directions

Preheat Cuisinart on Air Fry function to 380 F. Mix olive oil, old bay seasoning, cayenne pepper, smoked paprika, and sea salt in a large bowl. Add in the shrimp and toss to coat. Place the shrimp in the frying basket and fit in the baking tray; cook for 6-7 minutes, sahing once. Serve.

Speedy Fried Scallops

Prep + Cook Time: 5 minutes | Serves: 4

Ingredients

12 fresh scallops

3 tbsp flour

Salt and black pepper to taste

1 egg, lightly beaten

1 cup breadcrumbs

Directions

Coat the scallops with flour. Dip into the egg, then into the breadcrumbs. Spray with olive oil and arrange them on the basket. Fit in the baking tray and cook for 6 minutes at 360 F on Air Fry function, turning once halfway through cooking. Serve.

Fried Cod Nuggets

Prep + Cook Time: 25 minutes | Serves: 4

Ingredients

1 ¼ lb cod fillets, cut into 4 to 6 chunks each

½ cup flour

1 egg

1 cup cornflakes

1 tbsp olive oil

Salt and black pepper to taste

Directions

Place the olive oil and cornflakes in a food processor and process until crumbed. Season the fish chunks with salt and pepper. In a bowl, beat the egg along with 1 tbsp of water. Dredge the chunks in flour first, then dip in the egg, and finally coat with cornflakes. Arrange the fish pieces on a lined sheet and cook in your Cuisinart on Air Fry at 350 F for 15 minutes until crispy.

Savory Cod Fish in Soy Sauce

Prep + Cook Time: 20 minutes | Serves: 4

Ingredients

4 cod fish fillets

4 tbsp chopped cilantro

Salt to taste

2 green onions, chopped

1 cup water

4 slices of ginger

4 tbsp light soy sauce

3 tbsp oil

1 tsp dark soy sauce

4 cubes rock sugar

Directions

Sprinkle the cod with salt and cilantro and drizzle with olive oil. Place in the cooking basket and fit in the baking tray; cook for 15 minutes at 360 F on Air Fry function.

Place the remaining ingredients in a frying pan over medium heat and cook for 5 minutes until sauce reaches desired consistency. Pour the sauce over the fish and serve.

Crispy Crab Legs

Prep + Cook Time: 15 minutes | Serves: 4

Ingredients

3 pounds crab legs

½ cup butter, melted

Directions

Preheat Cuisinart on Air Fry function to 380 F. Cover the crab legs with salted water and let them stay for a few minutes. Drain, pat them dry, and place the legs in the basket. Fit in the baking tray and brush with some butter; cook for 10 minutes, flipping once. Drizzle with the remaining butter and serve.

Quick Shrimp Bowl

Prep + Cook Time: 15 minutes | Serves: 4

Ingredients

1 ¼ pounds tiger shrimp

¼ tsp cayenne pepper

½ tsp old bay seasoning

¼ tsp smoked paprika

A pinch of salt

1 tbsp olive oil

Directions

Preheat your Cuisinart oven to 390 F on Air Fry function. In a bowl, mix all the ingredients. Place the mixture in your the cooking basket and fit in the baking tray; cook for 5 minutes, flipping once. Serve drizzled with lemon juice.

Garlic-Butter Catfish

Prep + Cook Time: 20 minutes | Serves: 2

Ingredients

2 catfish fillets

2 tsp blackening seasoning

Juice of 1 lime

2 tbsp butter, melted

1 garlic clove, mashed

2 tbsp cilantro

Directions

In a bowl, blend in garlic, lime juice, cilantro, and butter. Pour half of the mixture over the fillets and sprinkle with blackening seasoning. Place the fillets in the basket and fit in the baking tray; cook for 15 minutes at 360 F on Air Fry function. Serve the fish with remaining sauce.

Delicious Fried Seafood

Prep + Cook Time: 15 minutes | Serves: 4

Ingredients

1 lb fresh scallops, mussels, fish fillets, prawns, shrimp

2 eggs, lightly beaten

Salt and black pepper to taste

1 cup breadcrumbs mixed with zest of 1 lemon

Directions

Dip each piece of the seafood into the eggs and season with salt and pepper. Coat in the crumbs and spray with oil. Arrange into the frying basket and fit in the baking tray; cook for 10 minutes at 400 F on Air Fry function, turning once halfway through. Serve.

Easy Salmon Cakes

Prep + Cook Time: 15 minutes + cooling time| Serves: 2

Ingredients

8 oz salmon, cooked

1 ½ oz potatoes, mashed

A handful of capers

A handful of parsley, chopped

Zest of 1 lemon

1 ¾ oz plain flour

Directions

Carefully flake the salmon in a bowl. Stir in zest, capers, dill, and mashed potatoes. Shape the mixture into cakes and dust them with flour. Place in the fridge for 60 minutes.

Preheat your Cuisinart to 350 F on Air Fry function. Remove the cakes from the fridges and arrange them on the greased basket. Fit in the baking tray and cook for 10 minutes, shaing once halfway through. Serve chilled.

Old Bay Tilapia Fillets

Prep + Cook Time: 15 minutes | Serves: 4

Ingredients

1 pound tilapia fillets

1 tbsp old bay seasoning

2 tbsp canola oil

2 tbsp lemon pepper

Salt to taste

2-3 butter buds

Directions

Preheat your Cuisinart oven to 400 F on Bake function. Drizzle tilapia fillets with canola oil. In a bowl, mix salt, lemon pepper, butter buds, and seasoning; spread on the fish. Place the fillet on the basket and fit in the baking tray. Cook for 10 minutes, flipping once until tender and crispy.

Sweet Cajun Salmon

Prep + Cook Time: 10 minutes | Serves: 1

Ingredients

1 salmon fillet

¼ tsp brown sugar

Juice of ½ lemon

1 tbsp cajun seasoning

2 lemon wedges

1 tbsp chopped parsley

Directions

Preheat Cuisinart on Bake function to 350 F. Combine sugar and lemon juice; coat the salmon with this mixture. Coat with the Cajun seasoning as well. Place a parchment paper on a baking tray and cook the fish in your Cuisinart for 10 minutes. Serve with lemon wedges and parsley.

Lemon-Garlic Butter Lobster

Prep + Cook Time: 15 minutes | Serves: 2

Ingredients

4 oz lobster tails

1 tsp garlic, minced

1 tbsp butter

Salt and black pepper to taste

½ tbsp lemon Juice

Directions

Add all the ingredients to a food processor except for lobster and blend well. Wash lobster and halve using a meat knife; clean the skin of the lobster and cover with the marinade.

Preheat your Cuisinart to 380 F on Air Fry function. Place the lobster in the cooking basket and fit in the baking tray; cook for 10 minutes. Serve with fresh herbs.

Meatless Recipes

Sandwiches with Tomato, Nuts & Cheese

Prep + Cook Time: 60 minutes | Serves: 2

Ingredients

1 heirloom tomato

1 (4-oz) block feta cheese

1 small red onion, thinly sliced

1 clove garlic

Salt to taste

2 tsp + ¼ cup olive oil

1 ½ tbsp toasted pine nuts

¼ cup chopped parsley

¼ cup grated Parmesan cheese

¼ cup chopped basil

Directions

Add basil, pine nuts, garlic, and salt to a food processor. Process while slowly adding ¼ cup of olive oil. Once finished, pour basil pesto into a bowl and refrigerate for 30 minutes.

Preheat Cuisinart on Air Fry function to 390 F. Slice the feta cheese and tomato into ½-inch slices. Remove the pesto from the fridge and spread half of it on the tomato slices. Top with feta cheese slices and onion. Drizzle the remaining olive oil on top.

Place the tomatoes in the fryer basket and fit in the baking tray; cook for 12 minutes. Remove to a serving platter and top with the remaining pesto. Serve.

Vegetable Fried Mix Chips

Prep + Cook Time: 45 minutes | Serves: 4

Ingredients

1 large eggplant

4 potatoes

3 zucchinis

½ cup cornstarch

½ cup olive oil

Salt to season

Directions

Preheat Cuisinart on Air Fry function to 390 F. Cut the eggplant and zucchini in long 3-inch strips. Peel and cut the potatoes into 3-inch strips; set aside.

In a bowl, stir in cornstarch, ½ cup of water, salt, pepper, oil, eggplant, zucchini, and potatoes. Place one-third of the veggie strips in the basket and fit in the baking tray; cook for 12 minutes, shaking once.

Once ready, transfer them to a serving platter. Repeat the cooking process for the remaining veggie strips. Serve warm.

Cayenne Spicy Green Beans

Prep + Cook Time: 20 minutes | Serves: 4

Ingredients

1 cup panko breadcrumbs

2 whole eggs, beaten

½ cup Parmesan cheese, grated

½ cup flour

1 tsp cayenne pepper

1 ½ pounds green beans

Salt to taste

Directions

In a bowl, mix panko breadcrumbs, Parmesan cheese, cayenne pepper, salt, and pepper. Roll the green beans in flour and dip in eggs. Dredge beans in the parmesan-panko mix. Place the prepared beans in the greased cooking basket and fit in the baking tray; cook for 15 minutes on Air Fry function at 350 F, shaking once. Serve and enjoy!

Cheesy Cabbage Wedges

Prep + Cook Time: 25 minutes | Serves: 4

Ingredients

½ head cabbage, cut into wedges

2 cups Parmesan cheese, chopped

4 tbsp melted butter

Salt and black pepper to taste

½ cup blue cheese sauce

Directions

Brush the cabbage wedges with butter and coat with mozzarella cheese. Place the coated wedges in the greased basket and fit in the baking tray; cook for 20 minutes at 380 F on Air Fry setting. Serve with blue cheese sauce.

Traditional Jacket Potatoes

Prep + Cook Time: 30 minutes | Serves: 4

Ingredients

4 potatoes, well washed

2 garlic cloves, minced

Salt and black pepper to taste

1 tsp rosemary

1 tsp butter

Directions

Preheat your Cuisinart Oven to 360 F on Air Fry function. Prick the potatoes with a fork. Place them into your Air fryer basket and fit in the baking tray; cook for 25 minutes. Cut the potatoes in half and top with butter and rosemary; season with salt and pepper. Serve immediately.

Roasted Carrots

Prep + Cook Time: 15 minutes | Serves: 4

Ingredients

20 oz carrots, julienned

1 tbsp olive oil

1 tsp cumin seeds

2 tbsp fresh cilantro, chopped

Directions

In a bowl, mix olive oil, carrots, and cumin seeds; stir to coat. Place the carrots in a baking tray and cook in your Cuisinart on Bake function at 300 F for 10 minutes. Scatter fresh coriander over the carrots and serve.

Garlicky Veggie Bake

Prep + Cook Time: 25 minutes | Serves: 3

Ingredients

3 turnips, sliced

1 large red onion, cut into rings

1 large zucchini, sliced

Salt and black pepper to taste

2 cloves garlic, crushed

1 bay leaf, cut in 6 pieces

1 tbsp olive oil

Directions

Place the turnips, onion, and zucchini in a bowl. Toss with olive oil, salt, and pepper.

Preheat Cuisinart on Air Fry function to 380 F. Place the veggies into a baking pan. Slip the bay leaves in the different parts of the slices and tuck the garlic cloves in between the slices. Cook for 15 minutes. Serve warm with as a side to a meat dish or salad.

Sweet Baby Carrots

Prep + Cook Time: 20 minutes | Serves: 4

Ingredients

1 pound baby carrots

1 tsp dried dill

1 tbsp olive oil

1 tbsp honey

Salt and black pepper to taste

Directions

Preheat your Cuisinart Oven to 300 F on Air Fry function. In a bowl, mix oil, carrots, and honey; gently stir to coat. Season with dill, pepper, and salt. Place the carrots in the cooking basket and fit in the baking tray; cook for 15 minutes, shaking once. Serve.

Colorful Vegetarian Delight

Prep + Cook Time: 25 minutes | Serves: 2

Ingredients

1 parsnip, sliced in a 2-inch thickness

1 cup chopped butternut squash

2 small red onions, cut in wedges

1 cup chopped celery

1 tbsp chopped fresh thyme

Salt and black pepper to taste

2 tsp olive oil

Directions

Preheat Cuisinart on Air Fry function to 380 F. In a bowl, add turnip, squash, red onions, celery, thyme, pepper, salt, and olive oil; mix well. Add the veggies to the basket and fit in the baking tray; cook for 16 minutes, tossing once halfway through. Serve.

Awesome Sweet Potato Fries

Prep + Cook Time: 30 minutes | Serves: 4

Ingredients

½ tsp salt

½ tsp garlic powder

½ tsp chili powder

¼ tsp cumin

3 tbsp olive oil

3 sweet potatoes, cut into thick strips

Directions

In a bowl, mix salt, garlic powder, chili, and cumin, and olive oil. Coat the strips well in this mixture and arrange them in the basket without overcrowding. Fit in the baking tray and cook for 20 minutes at 380 F on Air Fry function or until crispy. Serve.

Rosemary Butternut Squash Roast

Prep + Cook Time: 30 minutes | Serves: 2

Ingredients

1 butternut squash

1 tbsp dried rosemary

2 tbsp maple syrup

Salt to taste

Directions

Place the squash on a cutting board and peel. Cut in half and remove the seeds and pulp. Slice into wedges and season with salt. Preheat Cuisinart on Air Fry function to 350 F. Spray the wedges with cooking spray and sprinkle with rosemary. Place the wedges in the basket without overlapping and fit in the baking tray. Cook for 20 minutes, flipping once halfway through. Serve with maple syrup and goat cheese.

Herby Tofu

Prep + Cook Time: 30 minutes | Serves: 2

6 oz extra firm tofu

Black pepper to taste

1 tbsp vegetable broth

1 tbsp soy sauce

⅓ tsp dried oregano

⅓ tsp garlic powder

⅓ tsp dried basil

⅓ tsp onion powder

Place the tofu on a cutting board and cut it into 3 lengthwise slices with a knife. Line a side of the cutting board with paper towels, place the tofu on it, and cover with a paper towel. Use your hands to press the tofu gently until as much liquid has been extracted from it. Chop the tofu into 8 cubes; set aside.

In another bowl, add the soy sauce, vegetable broth, oregano, basil, garlic powder, onion powder, and black pepper and mix well with a spoon. Rub the spice mixture on the tofu. Let it marinate for 10 minutes.

Preheat Cuisinart on Air Fry function to 390 F. Place the tofu in the fryer's basket in a single layer and fit in the baking tray. Cook for 10 minutes, flipping it at the 6-minute mark. Remove to a plate and serve with green salad.

Cheesy Frittata with Vegetables

Prep + Cook Time: 25 minutes | Serves: 2

1 cup baby spinach

⅓ cup sliced mushrooms

1 zucchini, sliced with a 1-inch thickness

1 small red onion, sliced

¼ cup chopped chives

¼ lb asparagus, trimmed and sliced thinly

2 tsp olive oil

4 eggs, cracked into a bowl

⅓ cup milk

Salt and black pepper to taste

⅓ cup grated Cheddar cheese

⅓ cup crumbled Feta cheese

Preheat Cuisinart on Bake function to 320 F. Line a baking dish with parchment paper. Mix the beaten eggs with milk, salt, and pepper.

Heat olive oil in a skillet over medium heat add stir-fry asparagus, zucchini, onion, mushrooms, and baby spinach for 5 minutes. Pour the veggies into the baking dish and top with the egg mixture. Sprinkle with feta and cheddar cheeses. Cook for 15 minutes. Garnish with chives.

Cauliflower Rice with Tofu & Peas

Prep + Cook Time: 30 minutes | Serves: 4

Tofu:

½ block tofu, crumbled

½ cup diced onion

2 tbsp soy sauce

1 tsp turmeric

1 cup diced carrot

Cauliflower:

3 cups cauliflower rice

2 tbsp soy sauce

½ cup chopped broccoli

2 garlic cloves, minced

1 ½ tsp toasted sesame oil

1 tbsp minced ginger

½ cup frozen peas

1 tbsp rice vinegar

Preheat Cuisinart on Air Fry function to 370 F. Combine all the tofu ingredients in a greased baking dish. Cook for 10 minutes.

Meanwhile, place all cauliflower ingredients in a large bowl and mix to combine. Stir the cauliflower mixture in the tofu baking dish and return to the oven; cook for 12 minutes. Serve.

Chickpea & Carrot Balls

Prep + Cook Time: 25 minutes | Serves: 3

2 tbsp olive oil

2 tbsp soy sauce

1 tbsp flax meal

2 cups cooked chickpeas

½ cup sweet onions

½ cup grated carrots

½ cup roasted cashews

Juice of 1 lemon

½ tsp turmeric

1 tsp cumin

1 tsp garlic powder

1 cup rolled oats

Combine the olive oil, onions, and carrots into the Air Fryer baking pan and cook them on Air Fry function for 6 minutes at 350 F. Ground the oats and cashews in a food processor. Place in a large bowl. Mix in the chickpeas, lemon juice, and soy sauce.

Add onions and carrots to the bowl with chickpeas. Stir in the remaining ingredients; mix until fully incorporated. Make meatballs out of the mixture. Increase the temperature to 370 F and cook for 12 minutes.

Yummy Chili Bean Burritos

Prep + Cook Time: 30 minutes | Serves: 3

Ingredients

6 tortillas

1 cup grated cheddar cheese

1 can (8 oz) beans

1 tsp Italian seasoning

Directions

Preheat Cuisinart on Bake function to 350 F. Season the beans with the seasoning and divide them between the tortillas. Top with cheddar cheese. Roll the burritos and arrange them on a lined baking dish. Cook for 5 minutes. Serve.

Tasty Polenta Crisps

Prep + Cook Time: 25 minutes + chilling time | Serves: 4

Ingredients

2 cups milk

1 cup instant polenta

Salt and black pepper to taste

fresh thyme, chopped

Directions

Fill a saucepan with milk and 2 cups of water and place over low heat. Bring to a simmer. Keep whisking as you pour in the polenta. Continue to whisk until polenta thickens and bubbles; season to taste. Add polenta to a lined with parchment paper baking tray and spread out.

Refrigerate for 45 minutes. Slice, set polenta into batons, and spray with olive oil. Arrange polenta chips into the basket and fit in the baking tray; cook for 16 minutes at 380 F on Air Fry function, turning once halfway through. Make sure the fries are golden and crispy. Serve.

Garlicky Fennel Cabbage Steaks

Prep + Cook Time: 25 minutes | Serves: 3

Ingredients

1 cabbage head

1 tbsp garlic paste

1 tsp salt

2 tbsp olive oil

½ tsp black pepper

2 tsp fennel seeds

Directions

Preheat Cuisinart on Air Fry function to 350 F. Slice the cabbage into 1 ½-inch slices. In a small bowl, combine all the other ingredients; brush cabbage with the mixture. Arrange the steaks on a greased baking dish and cook for 15 minutes, flipping once. Serve.

Simple Ricotta & Spinach Balls

Prep + Cook Time: 20 minutes | Serves: 4

Ingredients

14 oz store-bought crescent dough

1 cup steamed spinach

1 cup crumbled ricotta cheese

¼ tsp garlic powder

1 tsp chopped oregano

¼ tsp salt

Directions

Preheat Cuisinart on Air Fry function to 350 F. Roll the dough onto a lightly floured flat surface. Combine the ricotta cheese, spinach, oregano, salt, and garlic powder together in a bowl. Cut the dough into 4 equal pieces.

Divide the spinach/feta mixture between the dough pieces. Make sure to place the filling in the center. Fold the dough and secure with a fork. Place onto a lined baking dish and then in your Cuisinart oven. Cook for 12 minutes until lightly browned. Serve.

Baby Spinach & Pumpkin with Nuts & Cheese

Prep + Cook Time: 30 minutes | Serves: 1

Ingredients

½ small pumpkin

2 oz blue cheese, crumbled

2 tbsp pine nuts

1 tbsp olive oil

½ cup baby spinach, packed

1 spring onion, sliced

1 radish, thinly sliced

1 tsp vinegar

Directions

Preheat Cuisinart on Toast function to 330 F. Place the pine nuts in the Air Fryer pan and toast them for 5 minutes; set aside. Peel the pumpkin and chop it into small pieces and toss them with olive oil. Place in the Air Fryer basket and fit in the baking tray. Increase the temperature to 390 F and cook for 20 minutes.

Remove the pumpkin to a serving bowl. Add in baby spinach, radish, and spring onion; toss with the vinegar. Stir in the blue cheese and top with the toasted pine nuts to serve.

Mom's Blooming Buttery Onion

Prep + Cook Time: 40 minutes | Serves: 4

Ingredients

4 onions

2 tbsp butter, melted

1 tbsp olive oil

Directions

Preheat Cuisinart on Air Fry function to 350 F. Peel the onions and slice off the root bottom so it can sit well. Cut slices into the onion to make it look like a blooming flower, make sure not to go all the way through; four cuts will do.

Place the onions in a greased baking tray. Drizzle with olive oil and butter and cook for about 30 minutes. Serve with garlic mayo dip.

Mozzarella Eggplant Patties

Prep + Cook Time: 10 minutes | Serves: 1

Ingredients

1 hamburger bun

1 eggplant, sliced

1 mozzarella slice, chopped

1 red onion cut into 3 rings

1 lettuce leaf

½ tbsp tomato sauce

1 pickle, sliced

Directions

Preheat Cuisinart on Bake function to 330 F. Place the eggplant slices in a greased baking tray and cook for 6 minutes. Take out the tray and top the eggplant with mozzarella cheese and cook for 30 more seconds. Spread tomato sauce on one half of the bun. Place the lettuce leaf on top of the sauce. Place the cheesy eggplant on top of the lettuce. Top with onion rings and pickles and then with the other bun half to serve.

Parsley Feta Triangles

Prep + Cook Time: 20 minutes | Serves: 4

Ingredients

4 oz feta cheese

2 sheets filo pastry

1 egg yolk

2 tbsp parsley, finely chopped

1 scallion, finely chopped

2 tbsp olive oil

salt and black pepper

Directions

In a bowl, beat the yolk and mix with feta cheese, parsley, scallion, salt, and black pepper. Cut each filo sheet in three parts or strips. Put a teaspoon of the feta mixture on the bottom. Roll the strip in a spinning spiral way until the filling of the inside mixture is wrapped in a triangle.

Preheat Cuisinart on Bake function to 360 F. Brush the surface of filo with olive oil. Arrange the triangles on a greased baking tray and cook for 5 minutes. Lower the temperature to 330 F and cook for 3 more minutes or until golden brown. Serve chilled.

Broccoli & Cheese Egg Ramekins

Prep + Cook Time: 25 minutes | Serves: 4

Ingredients

1 lb broccoli

4 eggs, beaten

1 cup cheddar cheese, shredded

1 cup heavy cream

½ tsp ground nutmeg

1 tsp ginger powder

Salt and black pepper to taste

In boiling water, steam the broccoli for 5 minutes. Drain and place in a bowl to cool. Mix in the eggs, heavy cream, nutmeg, ginger, salt, and pepper. Divide the mixture between greased ramekins and sprinkle the cheddar cheese on top. Place in a baking tray and cook in your Cuisinart for 10 minutes at 360 F on Bake function. Serve.

Zucchini Parmesan Crisps

Prep + Cook Time: 25 minutes | Serves: 4

Ingredients

4 small zucchini, cut lengthwise

½ cup Parmesan cheese, grated

½ cup breadcrumbs

¼ cup melted butter

¼ cup chopped parsley

4 garlic cloves, minced

Salt and black pepper to taste

Directions

Preheat Cuisinart on Air Fry function to 350 F. In a bowl, mix breadcrumbs, Parmesan cheese, garlic, parsley, salt, and pepper. Stir in butter. Place the zucchinis cut-side up in a baking tray.

Spread the cheese mixture onto the zucchini evenly. Cook for 13 minutes. Increase the temperature to 370 F and cook for 3 more minutes for extra crunchiness. Serve hot.

Cheese with Spinach Enchiladas

Prep + Cook Time: 20 minutes | Serves: 4

Ingredients

8 corn tortillas, warm

2 cups mozzarella cheese, shredded

1 cup ricotta cheese

1 cup spinach, torn

1 garlic clove, minced

½ cup sliced onions

½ cup sour cream

1 tbsp butter

1 can enchilada sauce

Directions

Warm olive oil In a saucepan over medium heat and sauté garlic and onion for 3 minutes until soft. Stir in the spinach and cook for 5 more minutes until wilted. Remove from the heat and stir in the ricotta cheese, sour cream, and half of the mozzarella cheese.

Spoon ¼ cup of the spinach mixture in the middle of each tortilla. Roll up and place seam side down in a baking dish. Pour the enchilada sauce over the tortillas and sprinkle with the remaining cheese. Cook in your Cuisinart for 15 minutes at 380 F on Air Fry function.

Vegetable Au Gratin

Prep + Cook Time: 30 minutes | Serves: 3

1 cup cubed eggplant

¼ cup chopped red pepper

¼ cup chopped green pepper

¼ cup chopped onion

⅓ cup chopped tomatoes

1 clove garlic, minced

1 tbsp sliced pimiento-stuffed olives

1 tsp capers

¼ tsp dried basil

¼ tsp dried marjoram

Salt and black pepper to taste

¼ cup grated mozzarella cheese

1 tbsp breadcrumbs

Directions

In a bowl, add eggplant, peppers, onion, tomatoes, olives, garlic, basil, marjoram, capers, salt, and black pepper. Lightly grease a baking tray with cooking spray. Add in the vegetable mixture and spread it evenly. Sprinkle mozzarella cheese on top and cover with breadcrumbs. Cook in your Cuisinart for 20 minutes on Bake function at 360 F. Serve.

Russian-Style Eggplant Caviar

Prep + Cook Time: 20 minutes | Serves: 3

Ingredients

3 medium eggplants

½ red onion, chopped and blended

2 tbsp balsamic vinegar

1 tbsp olive oil

Salt to taste

Directions

Arrange the eggplants on the AirFryer basket and fit in the baking tray. Cook them in your Cuisinart for 15 minutes at 380 F on Bake function. Let cool.

Peel the cooled eggplants and chop them. Process the onion and eggplant in a blender. Add in the vinegar, olive oil, and salt, then blend again. Serve cool with bread and tomato sauce.

Vegetable Spring Rolls

Prep + Cook Time: 15 minutes | Serves: 4

Ingredients

½ cabbage head, grated

2 carrots, grated

1 tsp minced ginger

1 tsp minced garlic

1 tsp sesame oil

1 tsp soy sauce

1 tsp sesame seeds

½ tsp salt

1 tsp olive oil

1 package spring roll wrappers

Combine all ingredients except for the wrappers in a large bowl. Divide the mixture between the spring roll wrappers and roll them up. Arrange on a greased baking tray and cook in your Cuisinart for 5 minutes on Bake function at 370 F. Serve.

Speedy Vegetable Pizza

Prep + Cook Time: 15 minutes | Serves: 1

Ingredients

1 ½ tbsp tomato paste

¼ cup grated cheddar cheese

¼ cup grated mozzarella cheese

1 tbsp cooked sweet corn

4 zucchini slices

4 eggplant slices

4 red onion rings

½ green bell pepper, chopped

3 cherry tomatoes, quartered

1 pizza crust

¼ tsp basil

¼ tsp oregano

Directions

Preheat Cuisinart on Bake function to 350 F. Spread the tomato paste on the pizza crust. Top with zucchini and eggplant slices first, then green peppers, and onion rings. Cover with cherry tomatoes and scatter the corn. Sprinkle with oregano and basil and sprinkle with cheddar and mozzarella cheeses. Cook for 10-12 minutes until golden brown on top. Serve.

Cumin and Cayenne Spicy Sweet Potatoes

Prep + Cook Time: 30 minutes | Serves: 4

Ingredients

½ tsp garlic powder

½ tsp cayenne pepper

¼ tsp cumin

3 tbsp olive oil

3 sweet potatoes, cut into ½-inch thick wedges

2 tbsp chopped fresh parsley

Sea salt to taste

Directions

In a bowl, mix olive oil, salt, garlic powder, chili powder, and cumin. Add in potatoes and toss to coat. Arrange them on the basket and fit in the baking tray.

Cook in your Cuisinart for 20 minutes at 380 F on Air Fry function. Toss every 5 minutes. Sprinkle with parsley and serve.

Jalapeño & Tomato Gratin

Prep + Cook Time: 35 minutes | Serves: 4

Ingredients

1 (16 oz) can jalapeño peppers

1 cup cheddar cheese, shredded

1 cup Monterey Jack cheese, shredded

2 tbsp all-purpose flour

2 large eggs, beaten

½ cup milk

1 can tomato sauce

Directions

Preheat Cuisinart on Air Fry function to 380 F. Arrange the jalapeño peppers on the greased Air Fryer baking pan and top with half of the cheese.

In a medium bowl, combine the eggs, milk, and flour and pour the mixture over the chilies. Cook in your Cuisinart for 20 minutes. Take out the chilies and pour the tomato sauce over them. Return and cook for 15 more minutes. Sprinkle with the remaining cheese and serve.

Chili Veggie Skewers

Prep + Cook Time: 20 minutes | Serves: 4

Ingredients

2 tbsp cornflour

1 cup canned white beans, drained

⅓ cup grated carrots

2 boiled and mashed potatoes

¼ cup chopped fresh mint leaves

½ tsp garam masala powder

½ cup paneer

1 green chili

1-inch piece of fresh ginger

3 garlic cloves

Salt to taste

Directions

Preheat Cuisinart on Air Fry function to 390 F. Place the beans, carrots, garlic, ginger, chili, paneer, and mint in a food processor; process until smooth. Transfer to a bowl. Add in the mashed potatoes, cornflour, salt, and garam masala powder and mix until fully incorporated.

Divide the mixture into 12 equal pieces. Shape each of the pieces around a skewer. Cook in your Cuisinart for 10 minutes, turning once. Serve.

Classic Ratatouille

Prep + Cook Time: 30 minutes | Serves: 2

1 tbsp olive oil

3 roma tomatoes, thinly sliced

2 garlic cloves, minced

1 zucchini, thinly sliced

2 yellow bell peppers, sliced

1 tbsp red wine vinegar

2 tbsp herbs de Provence

Salt and black pepper to taste

Preheat Cuisinart on Air Fry function to 390 F. In a bowl, mix together olive oil, garlic, vinegar, herbs, salt, and pepper. Add in tomatoes, zucchini, and bell peppers and toss to coat.

Arrange the vegetables in a baking dish and cook for 15 minutes, shaking occasionally. Let sit for 5 more minutes after the timer goes off. Serve.

Cheddar & Tempeh Stuffed Mushrooms

Prep + Cook Time: 20 minutes | Serves: 3 to 4

14 mushroom caps

1 clove garlic, minced

Salt and pepper to taste

4 slices tempeh, chopped

¼ cup grated Cheddar cheese

1 tbsp olive oil

1 tbsp chopped parsley

Preheat on Air Fry function to 390 F. In a bowl, add olive oil, tempeh, cheddar cheese, parsley, salt, pepper, and garlic. Mix well with a spoon. Fill the mushroom caps with the tempeh mixture.

Place the stuffed mushrooms in the basket and fit in the baking tray; cook for 8 minutes. Once golden and crispy, plate them and serve with green salad.

Korean Tempeh Steak with Broccoli

Prep + Cook Time: 15 minutes + marinating time| Serves: 4

16 oz tempeh, cut into 1 cm thick pieces

1 pound broccoli, cut into florets

⅓ cup fermented soy sauce

2 tbsp sesame oil

⅓ cup sherry

1 tsp soy sauce

1 tsp white sugar

1 tsp cornstarch

1 tbsp olive oil

1 garlic clove, minced

In a bowl, mix cornstarch, sherry, fermented soy sauce, sesame oil, soy sauce, sugar, and tempeh pieces. Marinate for 45 minutes.

Then, add in garlic, olive oil, and ginger. Place in the basket and fit in the baking tray; cook for 10 minutes at 390 F on Air Fry function, turning once halfway through. Serve.

Parsley Hearty Carrots

Prep + Cook Time: 25 minutes | Serves: 3

Ingredients

2 tsp olive oil

2 shallots, chopped

3 carrots, sliced

Salt to taste

¼ cup yogurt

2 garlic cloves, minced

3 tbsp parsley, chopped

Directions

In a baking dish, mix olive oil, carrots, salt, garlic, shallots, parsley, and yogurt.

Place the dish in your Cuisinart and cook for 15 minutes on Bake function at 370 F. Serve with garlic mayo.

Homemade Cheese Ravioli

Prep + Cook Time: 15 minutes | Serves: 4

Ingredients

1 package cheese ravioli

2 cup Italian breadcrumbs

¼ cup Parmesan cheese, grated

1 cup buttermilk

1 tsp olive oil

¼ tsp garlic powder

Directions

Preheat Cuisinart on Air Fry function to 390 F. In a small bowl, combine breadcrumbs, Parmesan cheese, garlic powder, and olive oil. Dip the ravioli in the buttermilk and then coat them with the breadcrumb mixture.

Line the Air Fryer pan with parchment paper and arrange the ravioli on it. Cook for 5 minutes. Serve the ravioli with marinara sauce.

Beetroot Chips

Prep + Cook Time: 25 minutes | Serves: 3

1lb golden beetroots, sliced

2 tbsp olive oil

1 tbsp yeast flakes

1 tsp vegan seasoning

Salt to taste

In a bowl, add the olive oil, beetroots, vegan seasoning, and yeast and mix well. Dump the coated chips in the basket.

Fit in the baking tray and cook in your Cuisinart for 15 minutes at 370 F on Air Fry function, shaking once halfway through. Serve.

Coconut Vegan Fries

Prep + Cook Time: 20 minutes | Serves: 2

2 potatoes, spiralized

1 tbsp tomato ketchup

2 tbsp olive oil

Salt and black pepper to taste

2 tbsp coconut oil

In a bowl, mix olive oil, coconut oil, salt, and pepper. Add in the potatoes and toss to coat. Place them in the basket and fit in the baking tray; cook for 15 minutes on Air Fry function at 360 F. Serve with ketchup and enjoy!

Garlicky Vermouth Mushrooms

Prep + Cook Time: 20 minutes | Serves: 4

2 lb portobello mushrooms, sliced

2 tbsp vermouth

½ tsp garlic powder

1 tbsp olive oil

2 tsp herbs

1 tbsp duck fat, softened

In a bowl, mix the duck fat, garlic powder, and herbs. Rub the mushrooms with the mixture and place them in a baking tray. Drizzle with vermouth and cook in your Cuisinart for 15 minutes on Bake function at 350 F. Serve.

Desserts Recipes

Summer Citrus Sponge Cake

Prep + Cook Time: 50 minutes | Serves: 4

Ingredients

1 cup sugar

1 cup self-rising flour

1 cup butter

3 eggs

1 tsp baking powder

1 tsp vanilla extract

Zest of 1 orange

Frosting:

4 egg whites

1 orange, zested and juiced

1 tsp orange food coloring

1 cup superfine sugar

Directions

Preheat Cuisinart on Bake function to 350 F. Place all cake ingredients in a bowl and whisk with an electric mixer. Transfer half of the batter into a greased cake pan and bake for 15 minutes.

Meanwhile, prepare the frosting by beating all frosting ingredients together. Spread the frosting mixture on top of the cake. Serve sliced.

Vanilla Brownie Squares

Prep + Cook Time: 25 minutes | Serves: 2

Ingredients

1 whole egg, beaten

¼ cup chocolate chips

2 tbsp white sugar

⅓ cup flour

2 tbsp safflower oil

1 tsp vanilla

¼ cup cocoa powder

Directions

Preheat Cuisinart on Bake function to 360 F. In a bowl, mix the egg, sugar, olive oil, and vanilla. In another bowl, mix cocoa powder and flour. Add the flour mixture to the vanilla mixture and stir until fully incorporated.

Pour the mixture into a greased baking pan and sprinkle chocolate chips on top. Cook for 20 minutes. Chill and cut into squares to serve.

Effortless Apple Pie

Prep + Cook Time: 30 minutes | Serves: 4

4 apples, diced

2 oz butter, melted

2 oz sugar

1 oz brown sugar

2 tsp cinnamon

1 egg, beaten

3 large puff pastry sheets

¼ tsp salt

Whisk white sugar, brown sugar, cinnamon, salt, and butter together. Place the apples in a greased baking pan and coat them with the sugar mixture. Place the baking dish in your Cuisinart and cook for 10 minutes at 350 F on Bake function.

Meanwhile, roll out the pastry on a floured flat surface, and cut each sheet into 6 equal pieces. Divide the apple filling between the pieces. Brush the edges of the pastry squares with the egg.

Fold them and seal the edges with a fork. Place on a lined baking sheet and cook in the fryer at 350 F for 8 minutes. Flip over, increase the temperature to 390 F, and cook for 2 more minutes.

Dark Chocolate Lava Cakes

Prep + Cook Time: 20 minutes | Serves: 4

3 ½ oz butter, melted

3 ½ tbsp sugar

1 ½ tbsp self-rising flour

3 ½ oz dark chocolate, melted

2 eggs

Grease 4 ramekins with butter. Preheat Cuisinart on Bake function to 375 F. Beat the eggs and sugar until frothy. Stir in butter and chocolate; gently fold in the flour. Divide the mixture between the ramekins and bake for 10 minutes. Let cool for 2 minutes before turning the cakes upside down onto serving plates.

Perfect Chocolate Soufflé

Prep + Cook Time: 25 minutes | Serves: 2

2 eggs, whites and yolks separated

¼ cup butter, melted

2 tbsp flour

3 tbsp sugar

3 oz chocolate, melted

½ tsp vanilla extract

Beat the yolks along with the sugar and vanilla extract; stir in butter, chocolate, and flour. Preheat Cuisinart on Bake function to 330 F. Whisk the whites until a stiff peak forms. Working in batches, gently combine the egg whites with the chocolate mixture. Divide the batter between two greased ramekins. Cook for 14-18 minutes. Serve.

Glazed Lemon Cupcakes

Prep + Cook Time: 30 minutes | Serves: 6

Ingredients

1 cup flour

½ cup sugar

1 small egg

1 tsp lemon zest

¾ tsp baking powder

¼ tsp baking soda

½ tsp salt

2 tbsp vegetable oil

½ cup milk

½ tsp vanilla extract

Glaze:

½ cup powdered sugar

2 tsp lemon juice

Directions

Preheat Cuisinart on Bake function to 350 F. In a bowl, combine dry ingredients. In another bowl, whisk together the wet ingredients. Gently combine the two mixtures. Divide the batter between 6 greased muffin tins. Place them in the baking tray and cook for 13-16 minutes.

Meanwhile, whisk the powdered sugar with the lemon juice. Spread the glaze over the muffins.

Homemade Doughnuts

Prep + Cook Time: 25 minutes | Serves: 4

Ingredients

8 oz self-rising flour

1 tsp baking powder

½ cup milk

2 ½ tbsp butter

1 egg

2 oz brown sugar

Directions

Preheat Cuisinart on Bake function to 350 F. Beat the butter with the sugar until smooth. Whisk in the egg and milk. In a bowl, combine flour with baking powder. Fold in the butter mixture.

Form donut shapes and cut off the center with cookie cutters. Arrange on a lined baking sheet and cook in for 15 minutes. Serve with whipped cream or icing.

Sesame Banana Dessert

Prep + Cook Time: 15 minutes | Serves: 5

1 ½ cups flour

5 bananas, sliced

1 tsp salt

3 tbsp sesame seeds

1 cup water

2 eggs, beaten

1 tsp baking powder

½ tbsp sugar

Preheat Cuisinart on Bake function to 340 F. In a bowl, mix salt, sesame seeds, flour, baking powder, eggs, sugar, and water. Coat sliced bananas with the flour mixture. Place the prepared slices in the Air Fryer basket and fit in the baking tray; cook for 8-10 minutes. Serve chilled.

Triple Berry Lemon Crumble

Prep + Cook Time: 30 minutes | Serves: 6

12 oz fresh strawberries

7 oz fresh raspberries

5 oz fresh blueberries

5 tbsp cold butter

2 tbsp lemon juice

1 cup flour

½ cup sugar

1 tbsp water

A pinch of salt

Gently mash the berries, but make sure there are chunks left. Mix with the lemon juice and 2 tbsp of the sugar. Place the berry mixture at the bottom of a prepared round cake.

Combine the flour with the salt and sugar in a bowl. Add the water and rub the butter with your fingers until the mixture becomes crumbled. Pour the batter over the berries. Cook in your Cuisinart at 390 F for 20 minutes on Bake function. Serve chilled.

Honey Hazelnut Apples

Prep + Cook Time: 13 minutes | Serves: 4

4 apples

1 oz butter

2 oz breadcrumbs

Zest of 1 orange

2 tbsp chopped hazelnuts

2 oz mixed seeds

1 tsp cinnamon

2 tbsp honey

Preheat Cuisinart on Bake function to 350 F. Core the apples. Make sure to also score their skin to prevent from splitting. Combine the remaining ingredients in a bowl; stuff the apples with the mixture and cook for 10 minutes. Serve topped with chopped hazelnuts.

French Apple Cake

Prep + Cook Time: 25 minutes | Serves: 9

Ingredients

2 ¾ oz flour

5 tbsp sugar

1 ¼ oz butter

3 tbsp cinnamon

2 whole apple, sliced

Directions

Preheat Cuisinart on Bake function to 360 F. In a bowl, mix 3 tbsp sugar, butter, and flour and form a pastry dough. Roll out the pastry on a floured surface and transfer it to the fryer's baking dish. Arrange the apple slices atop.

Cover the apples with sugar and cinnamon and cook for 20 minutes. Sprinkle with powdered sugar and mint and serve.

Classic Pecan Pie

Prep + Cook Time: 1 hr 10 minutes | Serves: 3-4

Ingredients

¾ cup maple syrup

2 eggs

½ tsp salt

¼ tsp nutmeg

½ tsp cinnamon

2 tbsp almond butter

2 tbsp brown sugar

½ cup chopped pecans

1 tbsp butter, melted

1 8-inch pie dough

¾ tsp vanilla extract

Directions

Preheat Cuisinart on Toast function to 350 F. Coat the pecans with the melted butter. Place the pecans in a baking tray and toast them for 5 minutes. Place the pie crust into the baking pan, and scatter the pecans over.

Whisk together all remaining ingredients in a bowl. Pour the maple mixture over the pecans. Set Cuisinart to 320 F and cook the pie for 25 minutes on Bake function.

Authentic Raisin Apple Treat

Prep + Cook Time: 15 minutes | Serves: 4

Ingredients

4 apples, cored

1 ½ oz almonds

¾ oz raisins

2 tbsp sugar

Directions

Preheat Cuisinart on Bake function to 360 F. In a bowl, mix sugar, almonds, and raisins. Blend the mixture using a hand mixer. Fill cored apples with the almond mixture. Place the apples in a baking tray and cook for 10 minutes. Serve with a sprinkle of powdered sugar.

Crumble with Blackberries & Apricots

Prep + Cook Time: 30 minutes | Serves: 4

Ingredients

2 ½ cups fresh apricots, cubed

1 cup fresh blackberries

½ cup sugar

2 tbsp lemon Juice

1 cup flour

5 tbsp butter

Directions

Preheat Cuisinart on Bake function to 390 F. Add apricots to a bowl and mix with lemon juice, 2 tbsp sugar, and blackberries. Spread the mixture onto the greased Air Fryer baking pan. In another bowl, mix flour and remaining sugar. Add 1 tbsp of cold water and butter and keep mixing until you have a crumbly mixture; top with crumb mixture. Cook for 20 minutes.

Quick Coffee Cake

Prep + Cook Time: 30 minutes | Serves: 2

Ingredients

¼ cup butter

½ tsp instant coffee

1 tbsp black coffee, brewed

1 egg

¼ cup sugar

¼ cup flour

1 tsp cocoa powder

Powdered sugar, for icing

Directions

Preheat Cuisinart on Bake function to 330 F. Beat the sugar and egg together in a bowl. Beat in cocoa, instant and black coffees; stir in flour. Transfer the batter to a greased cake pan. Cook for 15 minutes. Dust with powdered sugar and serve.

Gluten-Free Fried Bananas

Prep + Cook Time: 15 minutes | Serves: 8

8 bananas

3 tbsp vegetable oil

3 tbsp cornflour

1 egg white

¾ cup breadcrumbs

Preheat Cuisinart on Toast function to 350 F. Combine the oil and breadcrumbs in a small bowl. Coat the bananas with the corn flour first, brush them with egg white, and dip them in the breadcrumb mixture. Arrange on a lined baking sheet and cook for 8-12 minutes. Serve.

Vanilla Almond Cookies

Prep + Cook Time: 45 minutes + cooling time| Serves: 4

8 egg whites

½ tsp almond extract

1 ⅓ cups sugar

2 tsp lemon juice

1 ½ tsp vanilla extract

Melted dark chocolate to drizzle

In a bowl, add egg whites and lemon juice. Beat using an electric mixer until foamy. Slowly add the sugar and continue beating until completely combined; stir in almond and vanilla extracts. Line the Air Fryer pan with parchment paper. Fill a piping bag with the meringue mixture and pipe as many mounds on the baking pan as you can leaving 2-inch spaces between each mound.

Cook at 350 F for 5 minutes on Bake function. Reduce the temperature to 320 F and bake for 15 more minutes. Then, reduce the heat to 190 F and cook for 15 minutes. Let cool for 2 hours. Drizzle with dark chocolate and serve.